TEN BEARS

TEN BEARS

Miles Harrison Jr.
and
Chip Silverman

Foreword by Kweisi Mfume
President of the NAACP

Positive Publications

May 2001

ISBN: 0-967992-21-4

Cover and jacket design by Diane R. Baklor.
Cover photos, "Lacrosse Hall of Fame Statue" and "Holmes Hall" Copyright
    © 2001 by Diane R. Baklor.
Photographs within the text appear as credited, or through the permission of
    the authors and their colleagues.
Typesetting, layout, and interior design by Tom and Elizabeth Monteleone.

Printed in the United States of America

First Edition May 2001

A POSITIVE PUBLICATIONS BOOK
1-866-235-BOOK (2665)

*This book is dedicated to
the memory of*

*STANLEY CHERRY
JAMES "POOPIE" WILLIAMS
CLYDE TATUM
DANNY BELL
LEONARD SPICER.*

*Also, a special dedication to
RENÉE SILVERMAN
for her countless and tireless hours spent
working on* Ten Bears *for ten years.*

ACKNOWLEDGMENTS

We wish to thank Diane and Kent Baklor for their unwavering support of this project.

Thanks also to the following individuals for their invaluable contributions:
Brenda Royce, Andrea Savoy, Darnell Albarado, Roy Simmons Jr., Thomas Vennum Jr. for his book *American Indian Lacrosse: Little Brothers of War*, Andi Arenson, Courtenay Servary, Dave Raymond, Tyrone Scott, Tony Fulton, Jerna Jacques, Tyrone Jones, Wayne Jackson, Richard Hall, Tom George, Darrell Russell, Greg Wilhelm, Kim Willis, Rod Howard, Clarence Davis, William Bennett, Mike Walsh, Beautine DeCosta, Bob Litwin, Jeffrey Blumenfeld, Joshua Christian, The Lacrosse Hall of Fame, and the Morgan State Sports Information Office: Joe McGiver and Lamont Germany.

Special thanks to Arno Adams and Jimmy Adams for their support and enthusiasm for the Ten Bears from 1969 to 1975; and to Stewart Reichlyn for his contributions to the team from 1970 to 1973.

CONTENTS

FOREWORD

Ten Bears recounts the unprecedented accomplishments of the lacrosse team at one of the great historically black colleges, Morgan State University. Set in the racially turbulent 1970s, this powerful true story recalls the struggle faced by the team and its coach in infiltrating the antiquated and racially disproportionate world of intercollegiate lacrosse.

As an alumnus of Morgan, I can remember the inspirational effect the success of the Bears had on the campus and the community as a whole. Like seasoned soldiers, the Bears masterfully circumvented cultural barriers that sought to preclude their participation. Their unparalleled success represented a major turning point in athleticism. Their achievements, however, transcended the sports field, going beyond mere victory parties and coveted sports titles.

Perhaps unwittingly, the lacrosse team at Morgan became a symbol of cultural and communal advancement. The thought was: If a team of mostly black athletes had the fortitude and fearlessness to infiltrate—and dominate—the predominantly white arena of lacrosse, then other African-Americans had the ability to fight for justice and equity in forums that were previously inaccessible to them.

Ten Bears, written by two of the most distinguished gentlemen I've had the pleasure of knowing, has given the literary world a significant piece of work. Chip Silverman and Miles Harrison Jr. masterfully interweave the Bears' formative years and the players' personal hardships with the social tapestry of the times, shining a light on this little-known chapter in sports history. As one who was privileged to witness the Bears' remarkable triumph against seemingly insurmountable odds, I am delighted that readers can now share in the journey.

Every now and then the essence of the ordinary is captured in an extraordinary way. *Ten Bears* has found a way to reopen our eyes to the golden days of an era too long removed, when youth had its fullness and life was our chariot to the possible.

— *Kweisi Mfume*
President, NAACP

PREFACE

Ten Bears is the story of the lacrosse team at Morgan State, the first and only historically black college or university to participate in intercollegiate lacrosse in the United States. Coached by a white Jewish administrator for the Morgan Graduate School, this predominantly black team shocked the lacrosse community between 1970 and 1975.

This story is not just about a real-life sports fantasy, or about the only black college to ever compete against exclusively white institutions of higher learning, but much more. Born out of the riots of the late sixties, the Bears, named after the Morgan mascot, had a profound impact upon the nation's social and cultural consciousness. Yet *Ten Bears* flows with a resonance of young collegians at the precipice of adulthood trying to establish identities that could possibly open social and business doors traditionally closed to blacks.

The Morgan State Bears have been honored by the Maryland legislature and featured in the *New York Times*. The coach is reputed to be the only white person ever inducted into a Black Hall of Fame in America. And the players are now doctors, lawyers, legislators, teachers, coaches, civil servants, and businessmen. They are part of a very unique slice of Americana.

Ten Bears is a story that needed to be told for a number of reasons. First and foremost, it is a story of triumph against staggering odds—a black lacrosse team playing against the white elite of the lacrosse world. Second, it is a story of a coming of age—not just of the Morgan lacrosse players, but also of the game of lacrosse, of historically black Morgan State College, and of the people who passed through those turbulent times from the late sixties to the mid-seventies.

Lastly, there is no longer any predominantly black school in the country that plays men's intercollegiate lacrosse. Morgan was the first and only. The program was dropped in 1980, and no other black college ever took up the sport. So it is important that this story not be just a footnote of a unique athletic experience in the statistical pages of nonrevenue-producing sports in intercollegiate athletics; but that it has a life to be memorialized forever in the pages of *Ten Bears*.

The story recounted in *Ten Bears* is a personal one. I, Chip Silverman, was the team's coach and my coauthor, Miles Harrison Jr., was the star attackman. Miles was instrumental in convincing Morgan State's administration to start a lacrosse team in the first place. When I was recruited to coach the team—a short, white Jewish man with less than stellar athletic abilities—I thought I was an unlikely choice. But I was full of wide-eyed idealism and never doubted that I could help take the team to victory.

The story of the *Ten Bears* is true. When we decided to write this book, my coauthor and I realized that we would be counting on the memories of not only ourselves, but of the players and the people who passed through Morgan over 25 to 35 years ago. As a result, the episodes bear the tarnish of fading memories and the polish of ex-jocks embellishing their feats of long-lost athleticism. The same holds true for the activists and the militants rehashing their protests, sit-ins, and demonstrations.

The incidents, events, and characters in *Ten Bears* are based on fact. However, to avoid confusion and for the sake of continuity, we have taken literary license in some of the portrayals. For example, Football Coach and Athletic Director Earl Banks has been portrayed as the athletic director for the period of this book, 1969 to 1975. In actuality, he didn't become athletic director until 1973. He replaced Embra Bowie, who himself had replaced Ed Hurt in 1971. However, Banks was the individual who was approached by the students and faculty to begin a lacrosse program and who, inturn, approached me to organize a team.

In addition, there were several individuals who served as assistant coaches or consultants, including Goose Harrison, Schnoo Snyder, Gene Fusting, Stewart Reichlyn, Sheldon Freed, Jerry Schnydman, Steve Knepper, and Bob Frantz. Some served longer terms than others. However, in reconstructing past events, we have taken the liberty to use Schnoo Snyder in the role of assistant coach in most instances.

We're telling the story as we lived and remember it, but lacrosse historians and purists may find other examples of inaccuracies. If so, you're right, you win. It's like the sign in the pub near Morgan State that avoided arguments by acknowledging, "Your check is good. We don't cash checks."

— *MILES HARRISON JR.*
CHIP SILVERMAN

PROLOGUE

SPRING 1970

I stood there in the middle of the field wondering what to say next. What could I—a short, curly-haired, mustachioed Jewish guy—say to motivate the 29 young black men facing me.

No one had made a move after I'd ordered them—well, asked them—"Why don't we take a quick lap around the field . . . and stay off of the track."

The players were dressed in a variety of old football jerseys, worn and torn sweatpants and shorts, unmatched socks, and high-top cleated football shoes. They carried old, cheap-model wooden lacrosse sticks, some with patches of gut and leather missing from the webbing.

"After the lap, we'll do some calisthenics," I said, since none of the players had moved other than a few who stretched out or played catch.

I had been planning for this day for two months but was caught off guard by the team's reaction. I hadn't anticipated their apparent indifference to my instructions. I had been more concerned about practice routines, plays, conditioning, and scheduling. And definitely about my appearance. Disdaining the traditional jock-coach look—hooded sweatshirt, sweatpants, and oversized jacket with Morgan Football emblazoned on the back—I wore my dark blue work suit and shirt and tie. I had a whistle hanging loosely around my neck, my pants legs were rolled up twice, and I wore black Spot Rite low-top coach's shoes with rubber cleats. I'd dreamt about this "right" outfit for weeks: practiced nonchalance.

Damn it, I thought, I've been beat up before. If they don't respond in the next few seconds, I gotta go crazy.

"All right," I screamed, "what the hell are you waiting for? Get moving. Now! And if you motherfuckers don't run fast enough, we'll do it over. All day!"

The players' mouths dropped, but still no one moved.

"We got a game in two weeks," I said, still screaming but not as loud. "And you're a sorry ragtag group. If you want to be embarrassed by all those white preppy boys, that's fine with me."

I looked over at Stan Cherry, six-feet-five-inches tall and 235 pounds. Cherry was glaring at me, but I was sure I detected a hint of a smile.

"C'mon," said Miles Harrison Jr., a lithe attackman, "let's go!"

Cherry looked at Miles and grinned. He then took the lead and everyone followed.

When the lap was completed, Miles, Cherry, and two other experienced players—Val Emery and Dickie Hall—led the calisthenics. Afterwards, they broke into groups for ground-ball drills. Another lap followed.

As the team passed me, Miles whispered, "Nice touch, Coach. You can exhale now."

After practice, Cherry approached me by my car.

"Good practice, Coach. By the way, if you ever call me a motherfucker again, I'll kill you." A slight smile flickered across his face and was gone. "See you tomorrow."

CHAPTER 1

ON ATTACK: BALTIMORE AS A HOTBED OF LACROSSE AND CIVIL RIGHTS

FALL 1969

"Don't go to work today," pleaded my mother. "The schvartzes are rioting, and you work at a colored school. Are you crazy?"

"Mom, it's the safest place in town. Believe me. And besides, I've got to be there today. I'm organizing a lacrosse team."

I had been asked to form and coach the Morgan lacrosse team by default. Not only was I one of very few white academic administrators at Morgan at the time, but I was also the only person with any lacrosse experience.

While I knew the game and had played in college, I acknowledged that I had been a fair player at best. (Amazingly, as the years pass, athletes will embellish their past sports prowess, often becoming ex-post-facto All-Americans. With such exaggeration the rule, I must have been a truly pathetic player since I now called my ability merely "fair.")

Shocked and yet flattered that I was asked to coach a lacrosse team at Morgan by Athletic Director and Football Coach Earl Banks, I was amused at the irony of myself as a head coach.

As a high school and college player I had been very remiss at getting in shape and completing drills, preferring instead to just get the ball from a teammate and shoot, rather than play defense or hustle after ground balls. I was a very un-coachable, selfish, and lazy player.

Also, I was twenty-seven years old—young for a college-level head coaching position—and had no previous coaching experience; unless one considered my brief tenure at age twelve coaching eight-year-olds in softball.

While my coaching credentials may have been lacking, I had no reservations about working with a predominantly black team. I had relationships with the black community going back to my teens in one of the first integrated high schools in Baltimore, and then as a clothing salesman on Pennsylvania Avenue, the black business and entertainment hub of the city. Later, I was the only white teacher in a black elementary school and received my first master's degree at historically black Morgan State College. Upon graduation, I became assistant dean of the graduate school at Morgan State.

Despite my mother's reservations—a product of her own time and upbringing—I headed to the campus that fall morning full of optimism at the prospect of organizing the school's first lacrosse team.

○

Morgan State is located in suburban northeast Baltimore City. It began at the corner of Hillen Road and Cold Spring Lane. Rural Baltimore County could be reached within a matter of minutes by continuing out Hillen Road, whereas Cold Spring Lane cut across northeast and northwest Baltimore City for numerous miles. In 1969, urban blight was slowly encroaching upon these areas.

The Morgan State College campus was divided down the middle by Cold Spring Lane. On one side of the street were classroom and administration buildings, dorm rooms, and a student union center. On the other side were a physical plant, a field house, a fine arts center, and a football stadium. The campus stretched east for several dozen acres.

By the late '60s and early '70s, the community around Morgan was predominately white with black occupancy on the rise.

Located on a parcel of land known as the Ivy Mill property, Morgan was originally situated in the community of Laurelville. The college purchased the site when it was still a part of Baltimore County in 1917. It extended from Hillen Road crossing Herring Run, and was bound on the south by what is now Cold Spring Lane, but what used to be titled Grindon Lane.

On the original site, where Morgan's administration building is today, was the Ivy Mill Hotel that eventually housed classrooms and a library, and was renamed Washington Hall.

In 1918, the white community of Laurelville was incensed that the Ivy Mill property was sold to a "Negro" college. They attempted to have the sale revoked, appealing to the courts in Towson, the county seat of Baltimore County, and later challenging it all the way up to the State Court of Appeals. When these attempts failed, the citizen campaign turned to Annapolis, the capital of Maryland, to plead their case before the legislature on three occasions. Their argument was that a black school should not be allowed in a white community. When that argument failed, they proposed that no school should be built within five miles of what was then Towson Normal School, but is today Towson University.

The campaign grew ugly and included nasty letters to Morgan officials, and threats and demonstrations at the earlier site of Morgan State College in industrialized west Baltimore City. This building had been donated to Morgan College in 1881.

Morgan State College was originally the Centenary Biblical Institute, founded on November 27, 1867. The Institute was part of the Methodist Episcopal Church of Baltimore. Two years later, twenty students were enrolled for the 1869 academic year. And, in 1872, the charter of the college was amended to allow the admission of four African-Americans to the Board of Trustees. The first female students were admitted in 1874, and Susan H. Carr became the first female graduate in 1878.

The Centenary Biblical Institute changed its name to Morgan College in 1890 in honor of the Reverend Lyttleton F. Morgan, who was a member of the Board. That same year, the college granted permission to award degrees, and, in 1895, George F. McMechen received the first baccalaureate degree from Morgan College. Three years later, he graduated from Yale University Law School.

For a brief period of time, Morgan College established a graduate program. However, it was discontinued in 1926, lasting only three years. By 1933, the undergraduate school offered majors in ten fields.

Hughes Memorial Stadium was built during the Depression (in 1937) by unemployed laborers hired under federal government programs. The stadium was named for W.A.C. Hughes, who introduced football to Morgan College. That same year, Dwight O.W. Holmes was appointed the fifth president of Morgan College, the first African-American to hold that position.

On November 9, 1939, Morgan College was officially transferred over to the state, purchased from the Board of Trustees for $225,000. In 1948, the college established a Reserved Officers Training Corps (ROTC). That same year, Martin David Jenkins, Ph.D., a professor of education from Howard University, was appointed president. Jenkins began a tenure that would last over 22 years.

In 1964, an Urban Studies Institute was established at Morgan College, and a year later, Morgan reestablished the graduate school, offering degrees in five fields leading to Master of Arts and Master of Science degrees. And, in the summer of 1967, Morgan State College came under the jurisdiction of the Board of Trustees of Maryland's state colleges and universities. This was accomplished by an act of the Maryland General Assembly. Two years later, Morgan State College was ranked in a *Newsweek* magazine poll as one of the top ten African-American colleges and universities in the entire nation.

○

Morgan had a good reputation and high admission and academic standards, though in-state applicants were never denied admission. While getting into Morgan was easy for in-state residents, almost 70 percent of the Maryland freshmen would flunk out by their sophomore year.

Incoming students during President Jenkins' tenure always remembered his opening remarks at the Freshman Orientation Assembly: "Look to your right and left at the people next to you and shake their hands; 'cause they won't be here by your sophomore year!"

○

A large crowd crammed around the front of Holmes Hall, which housed most of the Liberal Arts Departments and the graduate school. Everyone was listening to a rabble-rousing student who was discussing the riots that were taking place in urban America, the death of Martin Luther King, and other racial and political issues. He was trying to inflame the students who were assembled on the steps as he read from his own radical poem *Pardon me, Mr. A merry ka*:

> pardon me for my activism
> i only wanted to vote
> pardon my militancy
> while I demand the right to work
> pardon me, again, Mr. A merry ka
> i only thought i was . . .

At the same time, I was strolling towards Holmes Hall. I had placed fliers around the school announcing a meeting to discuss the possibility of forming a lacrosse team at Morgan. The meeting was to be held in Holmes Hall.

Clarence "Tiger" Davis, the student "working" the crowd, was shouting, "And George Washington and Thomas Jefferson raped our great-great-great-grandmothers . . ."

I continued heading toward the crowd. As I approached, the students slowly parted, anticipating a violent confrontation. A scowl appeared on Davis's face. He stopped speaking. I nervously parted the milling students and climbed up the steps to the door of Holmes Hall. Recognizing that I did not mean to interfere, Davis's scowl turned into a smile and he gave me "skin" (what would be interpreted today as a "low-five") as I swiftly walked into the building.

As the door closed behind me, I heard Tiger say to the crowd, "Let's go out into the street and turn over some white people's cars!"

○

During the late '60s and early '70s Baltimore was changing. A city of neighborhoods divided by ethnic groups and cultural divisions, Baltimore had separate enclaves of Italians, Jews, Blacks, Poles, Greeks, Chinese, Germans, etc. However, when urban flight began and whites moved out to suburbia and rural areas in the surrounding counties, the city's ethnic landscape began to evolve. It was mostly a slow process, but certain areas, such as northwest Baltimore, experienced an accelerated urban flight as a result of "redlining"—when the political powers-that-be directed blacks to specific white neighborhoods.

When the riots began in the late '60s and continued into the early '70s, white flight escalated even more. The city became a racial powder keg. A generally harmonious city, despite its ethnic diversity, Baltimore was suddenly at a standoff. It was a tense, paranoid, fearful time with a divisiveness that rivaled the Middle East. A black face in a white neighborhood (or vice versa) was a dangerous risk. Although this was true throughout America, in a town like Baltimore, it was a surprise to many and a foreboding of things to come.

○

A lot of blacks, including small-time gangsters, knew me from my job on Pennsylvania Avenue, the hub of black Baltimore. I still sold clothes at the Piperack, a men's clothing store, on the weekends.

The owner, Phil, was measuring a customer who had tried on an oversized sport coat. Phil grabbed and gathered the coat in the back to tighten it as he said, "You couldn't take it a size smaller if you tried."

When the gangsters came in, Phil would lock the door and everyone who worked in the place would give them their rapt attention. I was once measuring the pants leg of a gangster when I noticed a gun strapped around the man's ankle. I didn't skip a beat, offering a semi-bell-bottom called the Continental Slit. The gangsters would buy thousands of dollars worth of clothing and leave, tipping everyone grandly. Curious onlookers snuck peaks through the front door. One of them was Tiger Davis.

For good luck after a great sale, Phil pissed all over the cash register. Everyone laughed, even the people outside who were looking in. A few minutes later, Phil told me, "Ring up the sale." I refused to touch the wet cash register until Phil promised me a new suit.

It was the suit I wore as I walked into Holmes Hall to meet with the lacrosse team candidates. The athletic director and football coach, Earl Banks, had asked me to feel out the possibility of fielding a lacrosse team. Banks was under pressure from the academic faculty to diversify the sports program.

○

At the meeting, I announced, "The Athletic Department has asked me to identify if there is any interest in a lacrosse team." Historically, Morgan had always been a football and track power among black colleges.

"If there is interest, we'll begin playing at a club level this spring." The club level in college was an unofficial or unsanctioned level, by intercollegiate rules, which usually preceded full varsity status and NCAA (National Collegiate Athletic Association) recognition.

I then asked the attendees about any lacrosse experience, and happily discovered that two-thirds of them had played in high school.

A big white guy, Joe Alex, told me that he was an All-State lacrosse player, and that he also played football. Another player,

Stanley Cherry, spoke out, "They call Joe the Polar Bear 'cause he's the only white guy on the football team." The team nickname was the Bears. Stanley continued, "For that matter, he's the only white guy in the black football conference!"

A young man named Miles Harrison Jr. stood and excitedly announced that he'd recently been accepted into the University of Pennsylvania's medical school, to the amazement of the other players. Acceptance to medical school after three years was an anomaly to most college athletes who usually took five to ten years to receive an undergraduate degree.

Harrison and his fraternity brother, Val Emery, both outstanding high school lacrosse players and academically strong athletes, had helped push the athletic director toward offering lacrosse.

From the back of the room, two very large football players from Texas asked in unison, "Just what the hell *is* lacrosse, anyway?"

"It's tough to describe lacrosse," I began, "except to say that it's a combination of basketball, hockey, soccer, and football. There is a lot of physical contact, although the finesse of passing the ball around and cradling it in the stick is one of the tougher parts of the game. There are numerous screens and picks set by players, and a lot of cutting and maneuvering for position. That's where the game appears like basketball.

"The field is somewhat similar to football, but is about ten yards longer and has goals at each end. The game consists of four fifteen-minute quarters, and has ten players on each team: three attackmen, three midfielders, three defensemen, and a goalie. The ball, two and a quarter inches in diameter, is made of solid India rubber, and is very hard.

"At the beginning of every quarter and after each goal is scored, the ball is put into play through a face-off in the middle of the field. Players, such as in football, can be body-checked as long as they're within five yards of the ball. You can't hit from the rear or below the knees. There is a lot of contact with the stick, and, in an attempt to dislodge the ball, you can hit an opponent on his stick and on his gloved hands. But there cannot be wild swinging or uncontrolled, repeated swings that are intentional to any other part of the body.

"Additionally, the helmets now protect more area around the face than they once did. There is a circle around each goal called the crease. Only the goalie or defensemen may occupy that area. If an attackman goes into the crease he can be penalized.

"There are two types of penalties: technical penalties such as off-sides or a crease violation, and personal penalties such as slashing, tripping, clipping, and so on. The penalties can range anywhere from thirty seconds to three minutes.

"The sticks are all different. Defensemen use longer sticks; attackmen and midfielders use smaller ones. The defensemen use a longer stick with a wider head in order to keep the attackmen as far away as possible. The goalie stick is extremely large with a big net to stop shots thrown at the goal . . ."

One of the Texas players stood up and said, "I still don't get it, but if it'll give us the chance to whup some preppy white boys' asses, count me in!"

I shook everyone's hand before approaching Cherry, who was huge and had a very menacing look. With a nasty scowl, Stanley introduced himself, "Name's Cherry, and I don't like white people."

○

Miles Harrison Jr. was brought up in black east Baltimore, and moved to black west Baltimore before his teens. His first experience with whites was as a student at Garrison Junior High, which was 75 percent white when he entered the seventh grade. By the time Miles completed the ninth grade in the mid-sixties, Garrison was 75 percent black.

He attended Forest Park High School in northwest Baltimore City which was 50 percent black. Miles excelled in academics and athletics and became an All-State football quarterback and lacrosse attackman.

As a high school sophomore, Harrison played varsity football. At the end of the season, the coach, Chuck Waesche, asked Miles, "What are you going to do this spring?"

"Play baseball. I'm a shortstop," Miles responded.

"No," said Waesche. "I've got a sport you'll be better at."

He handed Miles a lacrosse stick and a ball and told him, "Take it home and learn how to keep the ball in the stick by spring."

Harrison was the fastest kid in the school, and after he quickly mastered the stickwork, he played varsity lacrosse for the rest of his high school career.

An outstanding student and athlete, he could have chosen any Ivy League university in America—but he chose Morgan State. Miles chose Morgan for its racial legacy, his family history, and his desire to stay near home. The Harrison family tree was dotted

Attackman Miles Harrison Jr. *(Photo: Sid Brooks)*

with numerous M.D.s and Ph.D.s, and Miles's uncle was the vice president of Morgan State University.

The Harrison clan already had two generations of surgeons, and Miles pursued a premed path. His family ultimately became the second black family in the U.S. to produce three generations of surgeons.

Miles was naive about the dynamics of race because he had always experienced total acceptance due to his academic and athletic prowess. But as he grew older and was exposed to people in different environments, racism became more and more apparent.

It was obvious during his first two years at Morgan that Miles's goal of achieving early med-school admission would be met. But, his other goal of athletic achievement waned after freshman football season, where his only claim to fame was holding for extra points against Grambling University in the New York City Urban League game. That summer, in a football clinic held at the Baltimore Colts' summer facility at Western Maryland College, Miles faced the reality that 5'9" was too small for college football. Black college quarterbacks from around the country were at the clinic, each well over six feet tall. Players like Joe Gilliam, Jim Harris, and Doug Williams were there, throwing the football over 60 yards with apparent ease—just standing flat-footed and leaning backwards.

After the clinic, Miles and Coach Banks agreed that his football aspirations at Morgan would not be fulfilled. It was then that Miles began his campaign for the college to start a lacrosse team. An eternal optimist, he was sure it would happen. Banks was just as sure it wouldn't. Every new team meant a drain on the football budget.

At Morgan State, lacrosse was listed as an elective in the Physical Education Department, although there were never enough enrollees for a full class. Students who had played in high school were not allowed to participate in the lacrosse elective. This was another reason why a lot of former players urged the Athletic Department to sponsor lacrosse as a varsity team sport.

At the same time that these Morgan State student athletes were trying to get a lacrosse team established, there were other Morgan students who were attempting to create varsity soccer and baseball teams. A number of students who played baseball in high school tried to petition the Athletic Department to form a baseball team, but to no avail. Then there were the growing legions of foreign students, African and Middle-Easterners, who demanded a soccer team. They went so far as to establish a club team on their own. The foreign students were phenomenal players and would have probably received a tournament bid at any NCAA Division I or Division II level, but they had no political clout on the campus. Their club team lasted two years and then dissolved.

It didn't take much encouragement from me to convince the Athletic Department to go along with forming a club team following my meeting with the players. The academic side of the campus and Harrison and Emery's persistence had sealed the deal earlier, as long as a coach was found and there was sufficient interest by student-athletes.

SPRING 1970

It was the second day of practice and I was still a little uneasy—wondering how and when I would earn the respect of these players. Stanley Cherry was key. The massive athlete clearly inspired awe and dread in the other players. If he decided to give me a hard time, they would surely follow suit. But Stanley loved lacrosse and relished the contact, and his enthusiasm was infectious.

Midfielder Stanley Cherry during a break in practice.

I watched intensely as the team went through ground-ball drills—a practice that "separated the men from the boys." Of course, I couldn't use the term for fear of the word "boys" being misconstrued.

As I threw a ball out in front of three players, there was a rush to scoop it up and break clear of the opponent. Two were on the same side and the object was for one of the two to block out the opponent while the other went for the ball.

"I've got the man," one yelled out. "And I've got the ball," screamed the other. Every player would eventually be in the solo role during the half-hour drill.

Stanley Cherry didn't care if he had company or went solo—he was still going to punish someone. I felt a little sorry for midfield candidate Tony Fulton as he lay on the ground after a devastating check from Cherry.

○

Tony Fulton was the first college student in the Fulton family. His father came from South Carolina and his mother's family from Washington, D.C. His dad was the chief chef for the B&O Railroad. He always cooked for the president of the railroad and, on occasion, had also prepared meals for President Eisenhower as he rode the train.

Tony was born in an industrialized inner-city section of Baltimore called Cherry Hill. Soon after, the family moved to west Baltimore. Tony attended Garrison Junior High and by the ninth grade was five-feet-five-inches tall and weighed 180 pounds. The kids called him "Tony Ton." He suffered from low self-esteem and lacked confidence from the constant ribbing. So instead of going down the street to coed Forest Park High School with his middle-school tormentors, he went to the all-male City College High School.

Tony decided to go out for the wrestling team. He felt that not only would it toughen him up, it could possibly put the brakes on his weight problem. While he continued to be an average student, participation in sports built his self-esteem and confidence.

When Tony became a varsity wrestler, he had to decide whether to go up to the unlimited weight class, wrestle at 180 pounds, or to lose weight and wrestle at a lower category. He based his decision on the competition. At Mergenthaler High School there was a 360-pounder who wrestled unlimited. The guy had once crushed the breath out of Tony in a match during junior varsity (J.V.). Also at the 180-pound level was the feared Stanley Cherry of Edmondson High School. Tony decided to lose weight.

The wrestling coach, Bob Turpin, was also the J.V. lacrosse coach, and he recommended that Tony try out for lacrosse that spring. When the sport was originally introduced into Baltimore schools, few blacks played the game. But during the late '60s and early '70s, athletes were strongly encouraged by football, wrestling, or basketball coaches who also coached lacrosse to go out for this sport. The black players were motivated to try lacrosse in part because they wanted to prove they were as talented as the white players; but the primary lure was that they also saw this as a great opportunity to kick a lot of white guys' asses, just like they got to do in football.

Tony played crease attack (an offensive position in front of the goal) in high school and made the varsity team for his junior and senior years. When Tony's team played against Edmondson High, they all feared Stanley Cherry because of his reputation in high school sports. The first time they competed, Tony was playing in front of the crease and received a feed from behind the goal. He quick-sticked the ball into the net, but never saw the goal because Cherry had come up and hit him so hard that he temporarily blacked out.

As Tony looked up groggily, he heard Stanley. "Hey, motherfucker, you won't do that shit no more!"

Tony was hurt and had trouble playing the rest of the game. Edmondson destroyed City that day, as they would every time they played them in lacrosse. The players were always on the watch for Cherry, whom they dreaded and feared.

When Tony came out for the first day of lacrosse practice at Morgan State, he recognized Stanley Cherry and got a lump in his throat. While he was glad that Cherry was now on his side, he knew that in practice Cherry was going to be adversarial. Once, during ground-ball drills, Stanley was particularly wired. He was in a two-on-one drill, and as Tony went to scoop the ball, Cherry knocked him on his backside. As he looked down at Tony, Stanley said, "I told you two years ago not to try that shit."

O

After the first meeting of the lacrosse team that winter, Miles, Val Emery, Dickie Hall, Tony Fulton, Ben Kimbers, James "Poopie" Williams, and others began to bond. Some joined the same fraternities and concentrated on partying together. Others realized that there were political issues to deal with at Morgan State, not only international and national, but on the campus itself. When Morgan State's budget was not increased in fiscal year 1970, the students decided to protest. Busloads of students arrived at the Maryland capital. Annapolis had never seen so many black students. Students blocked the State House, the Senate, and the House of Delegates buildings.

Tony and some of the players were hanging around the steps, blocking the Senate Office Building, when they saw some very large state troopers about to confront them. Student leaders screamed out, "Put Vaseline on your face. They're going to Mace you . . . Put the girls behind you so you can protect them . . ."

The standoff was tense but, fortunately, the issue over the budget was resolved by Morgan President Jenkins and Governor Marvin Mandel. The students got back on the bus and there were no incidents.

Actually, there was one. Tony had borrowed Cherry's Edmondson High football jacket, and during the demonstration, it had somehow gotten soiled with Vaseline. When Tony arrived back at Morgan and returned Cherry's jacket, Stanley went berserk. He chased Fulton all over campus until Tony locked himself in a dorm room and hid there overnight.

○

The first week of practice was chaotic, with me trying to evaluate the ability of my experienced players while also teaching the fundamentals to the novices. Nothing was going right. A full-field scrimmage couldn't be held without at least three or four inexperienced players as part of a team; and it created massive chaos. These athletes, most of whom were football players, had to learn that they could not rely on sheer brute force in this game. Lacrosse required dexterity and agility.

A third of the players were causing mayhem—running into each other, throwing illegal checks and blocks, and tripping themselves and others with their sticks.

Finally, in disgust, I called the new players together.

"I'm gonna explain the game one more time," I said. "Then, tomorrow, we're going to go over to Johns Hopkins University to watch them scrimmage Mt. Washington Lacrosse Club."

"How's that gonna help us, Chip?" asked Harold Bell, a Texas native and offensive lineman who was 6'6" and weighed 270 pounds.

Coach Silverman and the Ten Bears at an early intrasquad scrimmage.
(Photo: DeWayne Wickham)

"Good question, Harold. They are two of the best teams anywhere. They play lacrosse at a very professional level. You'll watch how other defensemen play the game, and you'll get a good perspective of the whole field."

Another imposing figure approached, further dwarfing me. "I still don't understand something, Coach," said Bruce Caraway, Bell's home-buddy from Texas. He was 6'4" and weighed *only* 250 pounds.

"What's the key to the game?"

I picked up a lacrosse ball. "See this? This is the key. It's on the ground a lot during the game. The team that picks it up the most usually wins." I tossed it a few yards past the players surrounding him.

Harold Bell ran after it. For a man his size, he ran smoothly and swiftly. Bell scooped it up, after two feeble attempts.

"Doesn't seem that hard!" yelled Harold.

"Yeah," I said. "But if you don't scoop it up properly, you'll get hit. And the team that dominates ground balls takes some hits."

"Who the hell would hit us?" laughed Bell

○

Not many players ventured to the Johns Hopkins athletic field to meet with me and watch the Blue Jays (Hopkins' nickname) scrimmage the Mt. Washington Lacrosse Club. Of the novices to the game who did, most were awestruck at three things: the quality of the equipment, the organized play and stickwork, and the predominant whiteness of the players.

CHAPTER 2

A Very Brief History of Lacrosse: The Evolution and Devolution of the Sport

Historians trace the sport of lacrosse back to the 1630s, with many considering a game played in Thunder Bay, Ontario by the Huron Indians the first. Although widely played throughout the North American continent long before the Europeans "discovered" it, the game of lacrosse has received very little attention from historians; perhaps less than any other American team sport. And the game is one of the most poorly documented of American Indian traditions. Until the Canadians began playing lacrosse and made it their national sport in 1867, there were very few published accounts describing it. However, once the Canadians developed the game, its Native American roots became obscured.

The game is referred to in languages of various tribes as "men hit a rounded object" or "little brother of war." Contrary to popular belief that the word *lacrosse* came from the first French explorers or missionaries who felt the sticks the Indians used resembled bishops' crosiers, it was actually derived from games played in France with a curved stick, or "crosse," and a ball. Later, of course, the French used the term *lacrosse* to describe any Indian stickball game.

It is still today very difficult to discern the exact etymology for the terms the English and French used to try to describe the equipment and the game of lacrosse. In the Native American game, the expression "tying up" an opponent differs dramatically from today's strategy. In the original game, players dropped their sticks and engaged in violent wrestling matches. The near-naked conditions of Indian players made it difficult for their opponent to grab on to them and impede their progress. Many Cherokee players also rubbed themselves with eel skin or slippery elm to make their bodies slimy and difficult to hold on to.

Photo: Smithsonian Institution and *American Indian Lacrosse: Little Brother of War* by Thomas Vennum, Jr.

Early writings stressed the violent nature of the sport. In many Iroquois legends that discussed lacrosse, severed heads were sometimes mentioned as a substitute for balls. This symbolism has led certain writers to speculate that the game evolved from an ancient sport where the heads of battle victims were used as balls.

Of course, the North American Indian game resembled little of today's sport of lacrosse. Instead of ten players on each squad, it was usually played between two different tribes with as many as a thousand players on each team and with the goals separated by miles. The game was basically organized mayhem. People were killed and maimed while engaged in the contest. It wasn't as much a recreational or athletic endeavor as it was a celebration or a surrogate for warfare. And, many times, the game was used to settle territorial disputes among the Indians.

Photo: Smithsonian Institution and *American Indian Lacrosse: Little Brother of War* by Thomas Vennum, Jr.

Comprehending the Native American version of lacrosse is difficult without some knowledge of its magic and spiritual elements. Indian customs surrounding the game include sewing inchworms inside lacrosse balls; twisting bits of bat wings into a stick's netting; gazing by medicine men at miniature lacrosse sticks to predict the future; and burying famous players with their sticks.

The origin of and participation in lacrosse as a myth and as a sport were developed in accordance to the wishes of the ancient gods. Games were organized as part of religious holidays to mark the changing of the seasons or the positioning of heavenly bodies. Rooted in the mythology and oral history of the tribes that played the game of lacrosse were many legends of how it began. However, the primary legend was one of a mythical game between birds and land animals.

During the seventeenth, eighteenth, nineteenth, and twentieth centuries, lacrosse was also a social event for many Indian communities. It enabled tribes to reacquaint themselves, renew friendships, and indulge in summer powwows. The lacrosse matches gave them the opportunity to express kinship and social alliances at a regional or national level.

Perhaps the most famous lacrosse game took place at Fort Michilimackinac in 1763. A number of tribes in the Michigan area put aside their animosities to join in a concerted effort to defeat the English and capture the fort. The fort served as a pivotal depot for the English who controlled the rivers and the woodlands from this point. It was also a place where traders and the military could resupply. Whoever controlled the fort controlled the region.

The Indian tribes' strategy was to put on an exhibition of lacrosse outside of the fort. During the game, they would stage a mishap, throwing the ball into the gate. Once inside, they would attack the English. This well-conceived plan involved women hiding Indian weapons under their skirts and replacing them for the lacrosse sticks during the ensuing melee. The Native American strategy worked perfectly, and the Indians massacred the English soldiers and recaptured Fort Michilimackinac.

As an interesting sidelight, besides enticing the British garrison's curiosity into watching the lacrosse game, the possibility of betting on the game also lured the soldiers. Their proclivity to wager on this athletic contest helped to distract them from guarding the fort.

Gambling on the outcome of lacrosse was a serious matter, and the higher the bets the harder and more valiantly teams competed. Many tribes, such as the Cherokee, who were once slave owners, would actually bet their servants, as well as other tribes' children or women whom they had captured. The Dakota and Iroquois tribes also followed this pattern. Rematches were always scheduled to recapture losses, with the betting becoming higher and more desperate. The Jesuits documented such betting as early as the 1630s among the Hurons.

By the late nineteenth century, whites began betting heavily on lacrosse games, and their greed contributed to the decline of lacrosse among the Mississippi Choctaw tribe. Lacrosse matches had come to resemble cockfights—there was a lot of heavy drinking, unruliness, and violence on the field. Just about anything was bet on the games: land, rights to use land, goods, money; and even national disputes were settled on lacrosse matches. In present day Georgia, there is still a claim by the Cherokee that a huge tract of land is theirs as a result of beating the Creeks in a lacrosse game.

The Church got involved and expressed its opposition to Indian lacrosse, which Church officials considered immoral and uncivilized due to the gambling and violent nature of the game. In 1898, the State of Mississippi outlawed gambling at Indian lacrosse games, cockfights, and duels. As a result, the popularity of the game dropped significantly.

Women also participated in lacrosse in a number of fashions. Some competed on an intramural level, usually against other women. There were also games where women participated alongside and against men. However, in coed games, the Dakotas, for example, allowed the women a five-to-one ratio over their male counterparts. On another level, the women served in both a fan and coaching capacity. On the sidelines of the field, if their team were losing, they would encourage their spouses by whipping them with branches till they bled, all the while reminding them of the property at stake in the game's outcome.

Photo: Smithsonian Institution and *American Indian Lacrosse: Little Brother of War* by Thomas Vennum, Jr.

As tribal warfare dissipated for Native Americans, the game of lacrosse intensified, giving young men the outlet to vent their aggression. The Indian game allowed a number of physical maneuvers—tackling, wrestling, tripping, ramming, charging, slashing, and striking with the stick—that would result in disqualification in today's game. It was considered honorable for a young warrior to die playing lacrosse. However, situations occurred outside of the context of the game, usually as an aftermath of disputes, which resulted in much more violence. After a 1790 game in which the Creek defeated the Choctaw over the rights for a beaver pond, the Choctaw warriors launched a revenge attack. Five hundred Creeks were killed.

In the mid-nineteenth century the game of lacrosse began to flourish in Canada. By that time there were approximately 80 club teams playing in a loosely based Canadian Federation. By July of 1867, when the Dominion of Canada was established, the game of lacrosse was proclaimed Canada's national sport. Numerous contests were held between Indian teams, or tribes, and white lacrosse clubs, with the Indians always dominating. Canadian Indian teams played exhibition games not only in the United States, but also throughout Europe, even giving a command performance before Queen Victoria in 1876. They drew a great number of spectators and fan interest.

After the Civil War, lacrosse started gaining attention in the United States, primarily in New York State. The first white team in the United States, founded in 1867, called itself the Mohawk Lacrosse Club. (After that, Indian-inspired names such as the Redskins and Braves began popping up among non-Indian professional athletic teams.) In the 1870s, New York University was the first to produce a school lacrosse team.

As the sport of lacrosse spread, problems arose due to the different playing styles. The Indian game appeared less rational and less organized than the Canadian game. Objections were raised not only to oppose the violent nature of the Indian game, but also to restrict Indian participation at white clubs unless common rules were agreed upon. The white players obviously believed they were inferior to the Indians, so they eventually used new rules to disallow Indian players on white teams.

A technicality gave the whites the leverage they needed to bar Indians from their games. Due to poverty and unemployment among the Indians, they had to charge admission for the game, even if it only paid for travel. Thus, they were deemed professional and ruled ineligible to participate in national lacrosse championships in Canada, which the Indians had been consistently winning. As a result of the new rules, white teams began to receive most of the media coverage, completely overshadowing the Indians' participation. The game was now a white man's game; they had their new rules, controlled the spread of lacrosse, and had exclusive fan attention. To Canadian Indians this was just one more part of a systematic policy against the Indians, along with their land being stolen, their culture denied, and their nations eradicated.

O

Interestingly, there are not many Native American players participating in college lacrosse today or in recent past decades. The exception is the University of Syracuse, which in the '60s and '70s, and even the '50s, had very outstanding Indian players. Large numbers of Indian people throughout North America still play lacrosse, but there are two factions of lacrosse that have emerged: one played by the white lacrosse community and the other played mostly on Indian reservations.

Despite originating the game of lacrosse, Indians have received little if any recognition for this accomplishment. The Indian hostility goes beyond Canada and includes the "Baltimore Clique." Since a great deal of the college field game was developed in the Maryland area, with major lacrosse-playing colleges— Johns Hopkins, Maryland, and Navy—and some of the major equipment outlets located in Baltimore, the Lacrosse Hall of Fame was built on the Johns Hopkins campus. This may give the impression that Johns Hopkins or the Baltimore region "invented" or "owns" the game of lacrosse. As a result of the feelings of many Native Americans, the Lacrosse Foundation is trying to restore the proper recognition to the Indian game and is redressing much of the inattention to the Indian contribution. In front of the Lacrosse Hall of Fame, a bronze cast of two historic Indian players is prominently displayed.

A Cherokee from the Carlisle Indian School was elected to the Lacrosse Hall of Fame in the early 1900s, but it took almost 90 more years before another Indian was elected. After 201 inductees, Oren Lyons joined the elite group. He had played on the same team as the great Jim Brown at Syracuse. Lyons is a Faith keeper of the Onondaga Tribe, an artist, and the current coach of the Iroquois National Team.

Until the early 1970s, lacrosse sticks were made of wood and were manufactured by Canadian or New York State Indian tribes who carved and bent the wood, and made gut and leather for the stick. Today's sticks are made of plastic and weigh probably a tenth of what they weighed years ago. Very few wooden sticks are produced now, with most of the demand coming from the women's teams. The creation of the plastic stick effectively illustrated the white domination of lacrosse. It marked the final step in non-Indian control and development of the sport.*

○

Since there was almost a formal conspiracy to exclude the Negro from much of America's written history for years, very little appeared in books and references pertaining to the past of black sports participation.

Before the middle of the twentieth century, mostly people who had kept the stories and the statistics in their minds to pass along to subsequent generations imparted the history of blacks in sports. They became "oral historians."

Oral historians are a dying breed. Only through the efforts of black historians who diligently wrote their stories down have we been provided with a rich legacy of blacks in sports.

Such an individual is Rod Howard who was responsible for gathering a plethora of information for Arthur Ashe's voluminous sports anthology *Hard Road to Glory.* Rod was responsible for researching and investigating the past by word of mouth. For example, he uncovered virtually lost information about the first black lacrosse player—Albert F. Lewis, a Canadian goalie. By interviewing college statisticians and historians, Rod Howard was able to locate former players or fans who had witnessed games (or heard stories) from earlier eras and had reliable memories.

Lewis played on the Canadian National team in the late 1800s, and was a member of the Cornwall Club in the province of Ontario. The only black to play on a championship team in Canada, Albert Lewis was considered one of the best players in his day, and was mentioned in Joe Lally's book *Fifty Years of the Best* as one of the all-time greatest Canadian players.

References to the history of Native American and Canadian lacrosse are from Thomas Vennum, Jr.'s book American Indian Lacrosse: Little Brother of War, Smithsonian Institution Press, Washington and London, 1994.

There were no blacks mentioned in United States lacrosse sports history until approximately 1939 when Simeon F. Moss played for Rutgers University. According to lacrosse historians, Moss was the first Negro player on a college team. He was the only black anyone could remember who was photographed in a lacrosse uniform since Al Lewis.

During the early years of World War II, a black player named Lucien Victor Alexis Jr. played lacrosse for Harvard University. From New Orleans, he had followed his father, Class of 1918, to Harvard.

After World War II, lacrosse increased in popularity with blacks, and some of the better players had been encouraged to participate by their football and basketball coaches. However, none received notoriety until Jim Brown of Syracuse in the mid to late '50s.

O

In 1999, the Associated Press voted Jim Brown the greatest NFL football player of the twentieth century. ESPN also included him among the top 50 athletes of the past 100 years, placing him fourth. He is in both the College Football Hall of Fame and National Football League Hall of Fame. While his exploits on the football field are legendary, what is not as commonly known is that Brown is also acknowledged as the greatest lacrosse player of the twentieth century, and is also a member of the College Lacrosse Hall of Fame.

Jim Brown at the Lacrosse Hall of Fame Induction Ceremony in 1983. *(photo: The Lacrosse Museum & National Hall of Fame, and U. S. Lacrosse)*

At 6'2" and 235 pounds, Brown had an enormously strong upper body, and his thighs were double the size of a normal person. While it is said that he never got fatigued, it is also said that he never did calisthenics, never ran laps, and never even lifted weights. Since Jim played sports year-round, he never felt the need to work out. He also refused to be timed by pro scouts. Jim ran as fast as he had to, and if someone closed in on him, he always seemed to have the ability to just "step it up another notch."

Was he in shape? After college, he went into the Army and was stationed at Fort Dix in New Jersey. While there, he broke every physical fitness record on the books.

"Big Jim," as he was referred to at Syracuse, never missed a game or got hurt in his football career. This, despite being a "marked man" by college and pro teams. Opponents of his Syracuse teams always targeted Brown— "Gotta hit him late, gotta stop him, gotta double-up on him." Opposing alumni would sometimes give players money to "get" Brown. Jim knew he was a target and that there was often a price on his head. It wasn't always just because he was good; it was sometimes just because he was black.

Once, when accused of almost biting an opponent's fingers off in the pros, Jim responded, "How'd his fingers get in my mouth? He must have put them through my facemask. Keep them outta there!"

Jim attended school at Manhasset High on Long Island, a wealthy neighborhood where his mother worked as a domestic. He was the only black at the school. He excelled in athletics, averaging 32 points a game in basketball, and also played football, lacrosse, baseball, and ran track and field. As a teenager in 1952, Jim was a top-ten finalist in the U.S. Decathlon. He pitched a no-hitter in baseball and was approached by the New York Yankees. Although younger than most of his male counterparts in high school, Jim greatly out-skilled all of his peers—as if he were a man playing among boys. He was practically unstoppable.

(Brown was such a great all-around athlete that after his football career, while living in Los Angeles, he became an excellent tennis player, a scratch golfer, and a great roller skater. He also often played one-on-one basketball against Wilt Chamberlain, holding his own. Brown even considered boxing Muhammad Ali.)

A Manhasset and Syracuse alumnus, Ken Malloy, went to his alma mater to recruit Jim. However, the football coach, Ben Swartwalder, had had a negative experience with a black player and was not interested in recruiting any other black athletes. Malloy appealed to lacrosse coach, Roy Simmons Sr., and the track coach to pitch in for a partial scholarship. They agreed and Malloy matched their aid with his own money and community donations.

Brown entered Syracuse in 1953 as a 16-year-old freshman. When he tried out for football as a "walk on," the coach put aside all of his initial objections. Although Jim would experience friction with the football coach, quitting on occasion, his college football career there is still legendary.

Brown did not play lacrosse as a freshman because it conflicted with spring football practice, and he only participated sparingly during his sophomore year. He developed a special rapport with lacrosse coach Simmons and hung out with his son, Roy Jr., who started school in the fall of '54.

Jim Brown running in his Syracuse uniform in 1957. *(photo: The Lacrosse Museum & National Hall of Fame, and U..S. Lacrosse)*

Coach Simmons was also an assistant football coach and served as a go-between whenever Big Jim and head football coach Swartzwalder were at odds. Simmons was a Syracuse icon. He played football there from 1922 to 1925, and coached football, basketball, or lacrosse from 1925 to 1970. He died at the age of 94.

As a sophomore, Jim would run from the football field to lacrosse practice during the spring where he'd pick up his stick, helmet, and gloves from Roy Jr. "Big Jim" counted on Jr. to fix his lacrosse stick. "Get it right," he'd say. It was the era of wooden and gut sticks, which were very sensitive to weather conditions. Roy Jr. was always repairing the cracks in the stick and the netting. Many of his lacrosse opponents felt that Brown's stick was illegal because it was too short. In actuality, the stick was regulation length, but Jim's large frame made it appear smaller in contrast. The way he held the stick—with one hand and close to his body—made it appear even smaller.

During his junior and senior years, Jim excelled in lacrosse, putting more time and energy into the sport. He'd quit the basketball team because he couldn't get along with the coach. However, "Simmy," the lacrosse coach, always had a great rapport with "Big Jim."

Early on, lacrosse opponents underestimated Jim's skills. They believed he was just like other football players, casually playing the sport for conditioning for the football season. Hofstra's football and lacrosse coach, Howdy Meyers, was one of the first coaches to make lacrosse mandatory for his football team. While opponents feared the "moonlighting" football players' rough tactics, they usually figured that their lacrosse experience and stick skills would be lacking. Jim, who had picked up a lacrosse stick as an adolescent in Manhasset, never played lacrosse as if it were a secondary sport. He had superior stickwork, was ambidextrous, had a great shot, and no one could take the ball away from him. Jim also never lost a face-off.

Roy Jr., an outstanding lacrosse player himself, acknowledged that "Big Jim knocked me down more than anyone, ever!" For two and a half years, Jr. faced-off and went head-to-head against Brown every Monday through Friday at lacrosse practice. Big Jim and Roy Jr. not only hung out a lot, but also roomed together. Roy Sr. was like a dad to Jim and was always there for him.

Jim used to attend movies alone almost every night; he had early aspirations to be a movie star. Interestingly, for someone largely considered a loner, Jim was Class Marshall and also Student Head of ROTC.

Jim experienced racial problems off the field in college. One of his football teammates' girlfriends wouldn't even let Brown in her house when she invited the team over. He had to stay outside on the porch. And when Syracuse went to the Cotton Bowl in Texas, no hotel would take the team because of its black player, Brown.

As a result of racial prejudice, Brown was reluctant to travel south with the lacrosse team in 1956 during Spring Break. While his teammates scrimmaged against Navy, Maryland, and the University of Baltimore, Jim traveled home to visit his mom. Face-off duties went to Roy Jr., who had to go up against All-American football players from Navy and Maryland who dished out a pounding. When Jr. returned to campus he sarcastically said to Jim, "Thanks a lot!"

Brown was a "clothes horse" who found shopping for the right sized pants difficult. He had a 32-inch waist, but could never get his thighs into the pants legs. He eventually realized that he had to buy a 46-inch waist to fit his thighs. When the tailor altered the waist, the pockets met in the back.

By Brown's senior year, with no spring football practice, he was able to devote all of his energy to lacrosse. The Orangemen were pointing to the national championship, but knew that even an undefeated season would not be enough to wear the U.S. crown. Unlike today, where a tournament eventually leads to a single champion, up until the early '70s the best team was determined by a point system based on wins and strength of schedule. Since most teams played a regional schedule, usually an undefeated team from the Ivy League, the military academies, or teams from the South were selected.

Going into their final game of the season against a strong Army team, Syracuse was undefeated. The game was to begin following an important track meet versus Colgate. The track coach, who had initially contributed to Big Jim's scholarship, expected a return on his investment. He approached Coach Roy Simmons Sr. and asked, "Can I have Big Jim throw the discus and javelin? Six points for finishing first in those events could be the difference between winning and losing." Simmy reluctantly agreed.

Later, five minutes before the lacrosse game, Coach Simmons couldn't locate Jim in the locker room and sent a player out to find him. The player returned, informing the coach that Jim had already won the discus and javelin, and was now competing in the long jump. "Go get Big Jim, now!" ordered Coach Simmons. "Get him out of that hot sun." Just then Brown appeared, pulling his lacrosse jersey over his track outfit. He went on to lead the Orangemen to victory over Army and an undefeated season. The track team also won as a result of Jim's point contribution in the field events.

Jim Brown during a Syracuse game in 1956. *(photo: The Lacrosse Museum & National Hall of Fame, and U. S. Lacrosse)*

As usual, following the game, Jim Brown hung around to give interviews and sign autographs. Afterwards, he slowly walked across the field, turned 360 degrees, and walked up the stadium steps. When he got to the top, he turned, looked down, and waved goodbye to the stadium.

Undefeated Johns Hopkins University was declared national champion that year by a very narrow margin. The Syracuse team was devastated, and traveled down to the North-South All-Star game to root on Big Jim against Hopkins' best players. Brown's performance that day was unbelievable, scoring at will, and has grown to such epic proportions that it is compared to Wilt Chamberlain's 100-point basketball game.

Despite the best efforts of recruiters, Brown refused to sign a professional football contract until after the lacrosse season. He eventually signed with the Cleveland Browns.

A couple of years later Jim attended the funeral of Syracuse All-American halfback, Ernie Davis, along with his Cleveland Browns team, their head coach, Paul Brown, and the Syracuse Athletic Department. Afterwards, Big Jim announced to his teammates that he wanted them to meet his favorite coach. Swartzwalder of Syracuse and the almost mythical NFL coach Paul Brown looked up expecting Jim's acknowledgement. However, he said, "Simmy, meet my teammates."

When Jim Brown was inducted into the College Football Hall of Fame he was asked what his favorite sport was. "It's not even close. I love lacrosse. Unfortunately, there ain't no scratch (money) in that game."

O

In the late '50s, the lacrosse team at Baltimore City College High School was 90 percent Jewish. That team won the 1958 and 1959 Maryland Scholastic Association (MSA) lacrosse championships. It shocked the elite Gentile world where the former champions were always from the private schools: the Gilman's, the St. Paul's, the Boys' Latin's. As difficult as it probably was for the 1950s Gentiles to accept the Jews having championship teams and excelling at lacrosse, think of what it meant to the private school elitists by the late '60s when the blacks, having only been indoctrinated into the sport a few years earlier, fielded a team which vied for the MSA championship.

When the racial composition changed in the Baltimore City school system in the '60s, blacks took up the game of lacrosse. However, it was not generally an infatuation with the game that led to this migration. In most schools, the head football or basketball coach (and/or their J.V. counterparts) also coached lacrosse. These coaches would "encourage" their football and basketball players to participate in lacrosse every spring since they knew it was a way for them to stay in shape and also to pick up some additional athletic skills.

By the end of the '60s, there was only one public high school team that could compete for the MSA title with the private schools—Edmondson High School. It was these players who would go on to form the nucleus of the Morgan State College (later, Morgan State University) lacrosse program.

Morgan's Ten Bears were cast in the role of David as they entered the lacrosse world at the beginning of the '70s. The perennial lacrosse Goliaths in Division I, the colleges and universities with long histories of college lacrosse play, were Johns Hopkins University, the University of Maryland, Washington & Lee University, the Naval Academy, and the University of Virginia. In Division II, the dominant teams were Hobart, Towson State, Washington College, and Adelphi. Morgan State began competition as one of 120 teams participating in intercollegiate lacrosse. Eighty teams played in Division II and forty played in Division I.

O

Lacrosse became an Olympic sport for a brief period in the 1928 and 1932 games. Johns Hopkins University, which won or shared 42 national championships since it began playing in the late 1880s, was the United States representative and won or tied both of those Olympic competitions. Although the game continued to be a rough sport, it was played primarily by elitists and was sponsored by mostly private colleges of high academic standards.

Today there are over 230 colleges that participate in men's lacrosse, along with 140 women's teams, 900 high schools, and 200 club teams. Just about every state in the U.S. has some form of organized lacrosse, which is also played in 35 other countries. Maryland, Long Island, and upper New York State are today's hotbeds of American lacrosse.

CHAPTER 3

THE LEARNING CURVE

SPRING 1970

Morgan was playing their first ever lacrosse game against the Community College of Baltimore (CCB). Wearing torn football jerseys and using old wooden sticks, the Bears played surprisingly well. At halftime, a young man who'd been watching the game introduced himself to me as Wayne Jackson.

"You guys look pretty good, but you're lacking something," he said.

I asked him what that was, and he answered, "Me. You need somebody to get the face-offs and score a lot of goals."

Wayne walked away as a player named Dickie Hall strolled by. Laughing, I said, "What an ego. You should have heard what that guy just told me. He said that we needed him. I mean, who the hell is he?"

Dickie Hall explained that Wayne was one of the best players on his Edmondson High School team and as good as anyone in the whole region.

When the Morgan team went out for the second half of the game, I approached the referee, Matt Swerdloff. "Kid just came up to me and said he's the difference—he's what I need on this team. I mean, you know, some of these kids, they've got big egos, but they can't back anything up."

But Swerdloff confirmed what Dickie had said. "Oh no, Chip, Jackson can. I once saw him score eight goals in a game against Friends School. The game went into overtime, and he scored the winning goal. It was the greatest performance I ever saw in a high school lacrosse game. I went onto the bus after the game to congratulate Wayne, and I asked one of his teammates why no one seemed impressed. And the kid said, 'Wayne plays like that all the time.'"

CCB beat Morgan 9 to 7 in a closely fought game. Penalties, disorganization, and coaching miscues caused the "ragtag" Bears to lose their first encounter to a quality community college program, but I was delighted, nonetheless. The teamwork was lacking, but the desire was there, and the quality of play from Hall, Cherry, Harrison, Kimbers, Emery, and Alex was impressive.

O

The lacrosse team was using half of the football field to practice. Football players were doing spring drills on the other half, chiding Stan Cherry, Wayne Jackson (who had now joined the team), and some others for missing spring football to play lacrosse instead. Despite the ribbing, they were mesmerized as they watched their friends play lacrosse.

Hughes Stadium was built in lower than the surface of the campus. It appeared cavernous from the field looking up at the massive steps that served as seating for the games. Because the football team primarily used a running game—almost every play was "off-tackle"—Coach Banks purposely let very little grass grow on the field, which besides being barren, had rocks and bottle caps buried just below the surface. Players grew familiar with the "fast lanes" on the field and, after several weeks, they could follow them blindly.

Since at least a third of the lacrosse team played football at Morgan, home field advantage was definitely more than psychological. The "foots" taught the other players the nuances of the field and the retrieval of ground balls, an integral facet of lacrosse. This gave Morgan State a tremendous edge when playing in Hughes Stadium. Not many fans came out initially. Those who did were members of the vaunted football team—an ominous group of large and menacing-looking young black men.

I walked over and asked Coach Earl Banks why Morgan had never played lacrosse before.

"Actually, we did," answered Banks. "Bob Scott (the great lacrosse coach from Johns Hopkins) came over for a semester to teach the kids how to play. Unfortunately, one of our students, Willie Lanier (who became an All-Pro Hall of Fame National Football League player), got carried away one day and used a stick to club about five or six guys during a scrimmage. We had to cancel the class for the rest of the semester."

I jogged back to lacrosse practice and instructed James "Poopie" Williams on the nuances of "facing-off." Poopie was an older freshman who had served two military tours in Vietnam. A lot of the younger players teased him, calling him "Granddad."

Having recognized their skill, experience, and leadership qualities, I had Miles Harrison Jr., Wayne Jackson, Dickie Hall, Val Emery, and Ben Kimbers serve as "junior" coaches.

O

I had enrolled in Morgan State's graduate school in 1965 and received my master's degree in May of 1967. I attended full-time, which meant going to class every evening since all of my classes were held after six p.m. The dean of the graduate school, Dr. Frank A. DeCosta Sr., was impressed that I was teaching school in the inner city and going to school at night. The dean engaged me in friendly conversation on occasion, but I always thought he had ulterior motives.

More and more white students were enrolling in the graduate school, and the dean predicted (accurately) that Morgan would be one of the first totally integrated institutions in the country—50 percent white. Towards the middle of my final semester, the dean approached me and asked if I was interested in becoming assistant dean of the graduate school. I was eager to accept the position, more for the pay than anything else. As a teacher in the Baltimore City Public School system, I was making $4,400 a year. Dr. DeCosta promised me a starting salary of $6,700, major money in the mid-sixties.

Because I attended graduate school full-time, I was forced to take classes from a limited course schedule consisting of subjects of which I had very little knowledge or background. The courses included French Political Thought, France Under the Republic, and others relating to French social, political, and historical studies. Dr. David Levering Lewis, a brilliant academician and researcher, taught them all. (Ironically, in undergraduate school, I had had a fellow student take my final exam so I could complete a French language course. However, I was a great history buff and relished the programs of study.)

A year after I began working at Morgan State, Dr. Lewis went on a sabbatical to write the book *A Critical Biography of Martin Luther King*. During this time, I taught Lewis's Western Civilization undergraduate class and was a frequent guest lecturer for his French graduate courses.

Dr. DeCosta decided to take a semi-sabbatical leave during the 1969-1970 academic year to write a book for the Carnegie Foundation. It was to be the last academic book that ever had the word "Negroes" in the title. So I became acting dean of Morgan's graduate school for a year, even though the dean was around most of the time.

Although I came to recognize that some of the worst anti-Semitism was among Jews themselves, until I began working at Morgan, I was relatively unaware of the large amount of racism among blacks when it came to skin color. Sitting in for the dean on a faculty meeting for tenure, I couldn't believe the discussion that centered around the dark skin of an excellent history teacher. It appeared he would be denied tenure strictly on the basis of the shade of his skin.

The dean was a great tutor besides being a boss to me. He taught me everything he knew about administration, organization, planning, and management, and I absorbed all of it.

Aside from learning the technical aspects of college management, I relished my conversations with the dean on a myriad of topics related to black civil rights and sports history of the twentieth century. For the dean had lived it.

○

Frank A. DeCosta Sr. was one of eleven children born to an extremely poor family. DeCosta's father, a contractor, died when Frank was very young. The family struggled to make ends meet and all had to work. Poverty put them solidly in the lower class, but they were still part of the past generations of Charleston's elite society, and lines had been erased over time as to a person's standing and philosophy. In terms of status, blacks from Charleston, South Carolina tended to be conservative and elitist.

Education was the main motivation to young Frank who, because of his large family-centered upbringing, also became a very generous individual.

DeCosta arrived at Lincoln University in Lincoln, Pennsylvania during the Depression with very little money. While still working and completing his graduate education, he excelled in basketball and, later, played semi-pro and professional basketball. Frank even played a few times against the Harlem Globetrotters during their annual exhibition tour, and had an outstanding game against them once in Atlanta.

But the dean's main focus was academics. During his four years of undergraduate work at Lincoln University, he was elected president of his freshman, sophomore, junior, and senior classes; and was class valedictorian. DeCosta graduated with highest honors.

Dr. Frank DeCosta Sr., Dean of the Morgan State College Graduate School. *(photo:* The Promethean 1971, *Morgan State College Yearbook)*

He received his master's degree from Columbia University, and a Ph.D. from the University of Pennsylvania. The dean played a significant role in helping many black colleges and universities move from isolation into the mainstream of American education.

He was a distinguished professor and academician, and served as principal of a number of schools in the Deep South before becoming Department Chairman of Education and, later, Director of Instruction at Alabama State College.

After obtaining a Ph.D. in education, Dr. DeCosta married his wife, Beautine, from Savannah, Georgia in 1934. They had two children—a son, Frank Jr., and a daughter, Miriam.

A true believer in education, Dr. DeCosta gave financial assistance to numerous members of his huge family and other deserving students, enabling them to pursue advanced degrees.

The dean and his wife were working at Alabama State College in Montgomery, Alabama during the fifties when the bus boycott took place following the Rosa Parks incident. They attended the Dexter Avenue Baptist Church where a young man by the name of Martin Luther King was minister. The King family was very close to Beautine's family.

Beautine was an activist and had marched in Montgomery, Alabama civil rights protests. The dean did not participate out of respect for two things: one, the faculty of Alabama State College were not allowed to participate in demonstrations and protests of any kind; and, two, the Dean believed that civil rights could be obtained through federal legislation instead of protests.

Although not a "front-line" activist, DeCosta served as an advisor, researcher, and confidant to the civil rights movement. A great pragmatist and thinker, he was always the individual looked to by the leaders of the civil rights movements to run things by.

Former Supreme Court Justice Thurgood Marshall attended Lincoln University with Frank DeCosta Sr. Frank and Thurgood squared off against each other at debating team competitions. (The dean swore he always came out on top.) Marshall came to visit DeCosta when he was at South Carolina State College to discuss the landmark Kansas versus the Board of Education case.

After his tenure at Alabama State, DeCosta became dean of the graduate school at South Carolina State. In 1957 he joined the faculty at Morgan State where he was Professor of Education.

From 1961 to 1963, the Dean worked for the Agency for International Development in Kaduna, Nigeria. He helped train a staff of Nigerians to take positions as leaders in the field of education in their newly independent country.

When the dean worked in Nigeria in the early '60s, he would regularly have conversations with the first president of the newly emerging African nation, Benjamin Nnamdi Azikiwe, also a graduate of Lincoln. Dr. DeCosta had also gone to Nigeria to do research and to work on a proposal to develop an educational system for the nation.

A widely respected and distinguished scholar, his articles have been published in national journals. And in 1971, while on a semi-sabbatical from Morgan, he coauthored the book *Between Two Worlds: A Profile of Negro Higher Education,* which has become a monumental study on the growth and evolution of colleges founded by African Americans.

O

The dean and I had a complicated relationship. Though it was based on mutual respect, at times there was much more going on under the surface. I never knew if he was trying to manipulate me, especially once I let it be known that I was considering leaving Morgan to accept a job offer from the Maryland Drug Abuse Administration.

One evening, after hours, I was screwing an old girlfriend on the sofa in the dean's office. All of a sudden Dr. DeCosta walked in, switched on the light, went to his desk, picked up some papers, and strolled out. It was obvious he'd seen the woman and me, but said nothing. Naturally, I lost the mood, and the girlfriend asked, "Are you worried? Are you going to get fired?"

"No," I answered. "The dean needs me since the graduate school's half white. But, now he's got something on me. I'm getting married next month, and I'm afraid he's liable to lecture me about infidelity. Plus, he's pissed off that next fall I'm thinking about taking a higher paying job with the state as the Deputy Director of the Drug Abuse Administration."

O

The next day, the dean asked me to get him lunch at the drug store food counter up the road. It was the same order for three years. "Hamburger with raw onions and a vanilla shake."

I was expecting the dean to jump all over me about the earlier incident, but he didn't mention it.

I picked up Dean DeCosta's usual lunch order a few blocks west of Morgan State at a pharmacy/convenience store on Cold Spring Lane by Loch Raven Boulevard. It also had a dinette serving breakfast, lunch, and dinner.

Known as the Medical Center Drug Company, it had opened in the late forties. Ruby Stofberg was the colorful owner of the drug store. It was in the heart of an area called Northwood, a neighborhood not particularly enthralled with blacks or Jews.

Morgan State President Jenkins and one of his department chairmen visited Mr. Stofberg in 1950 to ask him if he would let blacks eat at his luncheon counter.

"That would be fine with me," answered Stofberg, and a few days later he began serving blacks in his drug store. The Northwood community responded with indignation. They began to picket Mr. Stofberg's store and later boycotted it. To show appreciation, Morgan State made sure that all of their students bought school supplies at the Medical Center Drug Company. Later, President Jenkins encouraged all Morgan students, faculty, and administrators to have their prescriptions filled only at Mr. Stofberg's establishment.

The other drug stores in the Northwood area were now losing money as a result of a lack of black business. They confronted Stofberg.

"Gentlemen," he said, "either join me and serve Negroes at your counter or you're going to have to close up."

The other drug stores acquiesced, basically ending the racial business restrictions of blacks in the Northwood community.

○

Because I had come up through the Baltimore City public school system and was familiar with their academic and athletic traditions, I was acutely aware of how most of the programs had deteriorated since 1960 when I graduated from Forest Park High School. Up until the late '50s, my alma mater sent over ninety percent of its graduates to four-year colleges—an incredibly high statistic for that period. Unfortunately, this percentage dropped dramatically by the end of the '60s.

Even though we were academic "winners," athletically we stunk. With the exception of the senior varsity players during the 1957-1958 academic year (when I arrived at Forest Park), the teams produced losing seasons on a very consistent basis. In my Class of June 1960, there were 460 students—400 girls and 60 boys. Therefore, if you were able to walk, every male student was encouraged to participate in as many sports as possible.

Though short and thin, I was a member of the football, basketball, and lacrosse teams. The cumulative records against public school competition during my fresh'-soph', J.V., and varsity years from the fall of '57 to June of '60 were nine wins and *ninety* loses; far beyond abysmal.

With the exception of a very good basketball team led by black players Rocky Armstrong, Maceo Dailey, and Clem Nixon in the early '60s (Forest Park was one of the first integrated schools to "start" five blacks on the court), Forest Park's sports programs continued a downward spiral until the late '60s.

But I wasn't unhappy—far from it. At least I got to play ball. I was able to develop *some* skills, even though sports and coaching were not Forest Park priorities. And I got to travel around the city, meeting opposing players from other ethnic neighborhoods who would call me anti-Semitic names and threaten to beat the hell out of me. Had I attended City College High School, which won 90 percent of their games, I would have been cut from every team, and not been exposed to the competition and diversity.

I actually enjoyed playing lacrosse against City regardless of the terrible beating Forest Park always received. Many of my friends from Baltimore's playgrounds and poolrooms were members of City's fabled '58 and '59 MSA lacrosse championship teams. Competing against them gave me a barometer of where my skills were. Of course, after losing 17 to 1 and 17 to 3, I realized I needed to vastly improve my game against the likes of Larry Levitt, Danny "Schnoo" Snyder, Stuart "Goose" Harrison, and Ray Altman—all of whom went on to become All-Americans.

○

Realizing I needed coaching help during the Morgan Bears' initial club season, I sought out Harrison and Snyder to assist me. Goose had a lucrative liquor wholesaling business and could only assist with the offensive unit once a week. On the other hand, Schnoo, an insurance adjuster, could work with the defense on a more regular basis.

A great natural athlete, Snyder put more emphasis on form and less on substance. He could handle the heavier wooden defense stick as well as the best attackman could cradle a small attack stick—maybe even better. As a 14-year-old, Schnoo picked up the nuances of the game immediately and had little patience for inept teammates. He was chosen All-State as a defenseman in 1958 and 1959 on that 90-percent-Jewish City College championship team.

Schnoo was also a very funny individual. His sarcastic wit was legendary among his contemporaries.

While he was a brilliant player, Snyder's impatience and sarcasm often made me regret bringing him on as the "volunteer" defense coach. Time and again as he taught positioning, stickwork, and strategy, he lost his temper, and the sarcasm flowed. His frustration mounted as Morgan's converted football players failed to grasp the rudimentary elements of lacrosse. Schnoo's reactions to fundamental relapses by the players created an atmosphere of animosity, distrust, frustration, and even hatred.

"Schnoo," I implored, "you can't berate the kids like this. It's counterproductive."

"They suck!" he shouted. "Except for a couple; and they'll never learn the game. You're wasting your time. And mine."

Schnoo Snyder was among those great athletes who expected the players they were coaching to already possess the same abilities that they themselves had had when they began playing. It's why most superstar players from college and professional ranks rarely make good coaches. They haven't got the patience, to begin with, to stress the basics and fundamentals of the game and then reinforce it over and over again. And, as a result, kids with potential who need time to adjust and pick up the sport become frustrated and fearful of making mistakes. They either quit or never develop to their fullest potential because there is little or no emphasis on fundamentals, and the patience or tolerance level of coaching is nil.

As the short club season progressed, two players quit in tears after tirades from Snyder. And two others slashed the front tires of his car after practice.

Schnoo would get so pissed off at times that he would leave the field in the middle of practice or a game and go home. Although, other times, his early leave-taking was just to catch the last few races at Pimlico Race Track. Schnoo loved to wager on the ponies.

○

The reputation of Morgan's lacrosse players was beginning to spread. After a shaky start, the Ten Bears began to come together collectively and individually. Wayne Jackson's size, stickwork, spin moves, and shooting skills were compared to pro basketball's Earl Monroe. (Monroe had played in the late sixties against Morgan State when he attended Winston-Salem College and was called "Black Jesus.") Stan Cherry was already making his mark as a feared linebacker for the Bears, and his ferocity on the lacrosse field sent shivers up the spines of opponents.

Stan liked to shoot the lacrosse ball at players' faces. His follow-through often caused the stick to come down on opposing players' kneecaps. He kept a running score of how many kneecaps he had damaged since high school. From fear and painful experience, opposing players often just ducked when Cherry was in possession of the ball.

Crease attackman Richard "Dickie" Hall. *(photo: Sid Brooks)*

And there was the ROTC leader and former Edmondson High great (as were Wayne and Stan), the high-scoring and tenacious Dickie Hall. Nicknamed the "Mud-Puppy" because he played well in sloppy weather, he was the consummate ground-ball man. He played crease attack with a small defense stick, scooped up every loose ball, and scored dozens of "garbage" goals (goals not artfully thrown or kicked in). Although his game appeared awkward, he was a combination unsung hero and most valuable player year in and year out.

With a few weeks of practice under their belts, the Ten Bears defeated Catonsville Community College, Towson State Frosh, and

Johns Hopkins Frosh. Not exactly "Murderers' Row," but quality competition for a first-year team playing in the Baltimore metropolitan area.

○

Cities, towns, and college campuses were experiencing turbulent times during the early months of 1970. Unrest, tension, and short tempers marked the landscapes of University of Maryland at College Park, Johns Hopkins University, and Morgan State College, as well as Baltimore City, Cambridge on the Eastern Shore, and Bel Air in Harford County.

It was individuals like Clarence Tiger Davis who kept social and racial issues at a boiling point. College campuses were an adjunct to the black community, and much of the leadership came from the campuses.

Not only did Tiger speak to large rallies at Morgan, he also conducted classes on the cause and the struggle anywhere around the school—even if there were only two or three students interested.

Schnoo and I observed such an event as we left practice and walked to my car.

"America is practicing genocide," said Tiger while speaking to a couple of students near the football field. "There are many racists in this community. White folks are subconsciously evil."

Tiger finished, stood up, and walked over to me. He introduced himself to Schnoo, whom he had played football against in high school.

"Where you guys headed?" asked Tiger. "There's a great party at this pad where I'm staying. Lots of pretty and liberated women will be there."

"Bullshit," I said. "You just need a ride up to Bel Air."

"That's true, Chip. But there are a lot of brothers you should meet; and also William Kunstler is staying with us. He's defending Rap Brown along with some other attorneys. I'll introduce ya."

Although I could sense that Schnoo wasn't interested, I convinced him that we'd only stay for a half-hour, and afterwards, I would buy him dinner.

The ride to 576 Revolution Street in Bel Air took 50 minutes. The house was huge and had numerous bedrooms. It was across the street from Harford Memorial Hospital, from where it was later revealed that the FBI had set up surveillance of the place. (They had also bugged the telephones.)

Bel Air, Maryland had been chosen as the site for the trial of H. Rap Brown during the "Black Insurrection" (as Tiger referred to the riots in Cambridge, Maryland). H. Rap Brown had been charged with arson and incitement to riot.

Initially, Brown came to prominence when he replaced Stokely Carmichael as chairman of SNCC (Student Nonviolent Coordinating Committee) in May of 1967. Although originally a nonviolent civil rights organization, SNCC became one of the movement's most militant organizations. Less than a year later, Brown was named Minister of Justice in the Black Panther Party.

Considered one of the angriest young blacks in an era of anger, Brown toured the United States espousing Black Power, opposing the Vietnam War, and denouncing the nonviolent approach to obtaining civil rights. He called on blacks to arm themselves, saying, "Violence is as American as cherry pie." In July of 1967, he was charged by the State of Maryland with inciting a riot in the small Eastern Shore town of Cambridge in the county of Dorchester.

The legal maneuvering of Brown's counterculture attorney, William Kunstler, helped to delay the trial scheduled in Cambridge for over two years—until a bomb exploded in the Dorchester County Courthouse. The trial was subsequently moved to the Harford County town of Bel Air.

Schnoo and I met several of Rap Brown's defense team, including Howard Moore from Atlanta, who was also the attorney for famous West Coast activist, Angela Davis. When Tiger took us in to meet William Kunstler, the nationally renowned radical lawyer, he was in bed with a pretty woman and had little time for talk. Schnoo nudged me to notice how heavily armed many of the home's occupants were, and a couple minutes later, we interrupted Tiger on the phone to say goodbye.

Tiger ignored us. He had just received a call telling him "a couple of black brothers were blown up in a car down the road."

By the time Tiger and two carloads of heavily armed activists had left, Schnoo and I were speeding back to Baltimore.

That night on the television it was reported that two blacks— Ralph Featherstone and William Che Payne—had been killed in a car explosion. There were conflicting accounts as to whether the car's occupants were carrying explosives or Klansmen had thrown a bomb into the automobile. Featherstone had been the organizer of the Mississippi Freedom Campaign. He was cremated and his ashes were sent to Africa.

Tiger insisted, "Featherstone and Payne were ambushed by Birchers or the Klan!"

Tiger Davis and Attorney William Kuntsler listen as Colonel Smith of the Maryland State Police explains the bomb damage to the car in Bel Air. *(photo: the* Harford Democrat*)*

○

Historically, when a new team or sport emerged at a college or university, it took years to establish a winning tradition and/or a nucleus or pipeline from a high school to continually refresh the team with new high-caliber talent. But the lacrosse team was fortunate at Morgan due to the influx of athletes from Edmondson High School. Dickie Hall, Wayne Jackson, and Stanley Cherry were three of the guys who led the way for the "Ten Bears."

The Edmondson High School players brought to Morgan lacrosse skills and a winning attitude. They were not awed by the reputations of opposing teams since they had beaten the best in the Maryland public and private school system for three years. And they knew that the best players from Maryland had become the best at most of the major colleges around the country.

○

Richard "Dickie" Hall attended Edmondson High School from

the fall of '66 to the spring of '69. He played lacrosse for three years, played one year of J.V. football, and wrestled varsity for two seasons.

The Halls moved to the Edmondson Village area in west Baltimore in 1962. Edmondson Village and the newly opened Edmondson High School, built in 1958, went from predominantly white in 1963 to integrated by 1966, and to 95 percent black in 1969.

Dickie's family moved from South Carolina to Baltimore in the mid-fifties. Initially, they lived in an apartment in a lower-class neighborhood in the city. Hall's father was a veteran of the Korean War, and he, like many poor black families, had migrated north in hopes of a better life. There was very little work in the economically depressed South at the time for blacks. Dickie's dad got a job at Bethlehem Steel, and his mother worked in a tomato-canning factory.

Dickie played stickball and a game called "Tin Can Johnnie" when he was growing up in the streets of Baltimore. Tin Can Johnnie was similar to Hide 'n' Seek except you would take a tin can and throw it down a dark alley. Whoever was "it" would have to find the tin can first and then find the other kids who were hiding. Dickie attended Harlem Park Junior High and then Edmondson High School when the family moved.

As a sophomore, Dickie tried out for the junior varsity football team, which is where he first met Stanley Cherry, a tall, slim teenager, very strong and very aggressive. Dickie and Stan became instant competitors and had numerous battles. Although they respected each other's talents, Stanley often picked on Dickie.

Following the football season, Dickie and Stanley both became members of the varsity wrestling team. But, in the spring when Stanley went out for lacrosse, Dickie tried out for the baseball team. He saw himself as a right fielder. Unfortunately, Dickie did not have the recreational league experience that so many of the other players had, and he was cut.

He came home one evening and saw a lacrosse stick in the hallway that his uncle, also a high school student, had brought home. The uncle had tried out for the lacrosse team but quit after two days. Dickie took the stick and decided to try out for the junior varsity. He instinctively picked the game up; so well that the coaches put him on the varsity team by his sophomore year.

At the time, Edmondson High School was experiencing its halcyon days of producing great athletic teams. Just about every

Edmondson sports team vied for the city or what was called the Maryland Scholastic Association Championships regardless of the division in which they played.

Wayne Jackson was already a varsity lacrosse player. He was a year ahead of Dickie; and Morgan Holley, who would also go on to play for the Bears, was a senior. In addition, the team included the Magwood brothers: Johnny and Ralph, Maurice Dorsey, and Alonzo Chavis who was an outstanding lineman on the football team as well.

The '67 lacrosse team won the public school title led by Johnny Magwood and Wayne Jackson. David Lewis, Stanley Cherry, and Alonzo Chavis played defense. The '68 and '69 teams defeated most of the outstanding private schools.

The players were initially coached and taught fundamental lacrosse by Coach Augie Waibel, who was also the football coach. He used many of his football players for lacrosse, realizing that they were good athletes, and that lacrosse gave them additional skills and helped them stay in condition year-round. Their size also made them an intimidating force in lacrosse.

To develop their skills even more, Hall and others would go to the recreation center at a nearby park to play lacrosse after practice. Dickie had an enormous drive to excel at lacrosse. When he first started going to the park, he'd throw the ball against a back wall of the "rec" center aiming for the door. He was lucky if he could even hit the wall. Eventually, not only could he hit the door, but he learned to control the stick well enough that he could hit the doorknob or the keyhole. It took him three years to get to that point.

He played midfield mostly, but during his senior year he also played crease attack. Dickie developed a "nose" for the ball since he realized that, with such top competitors, he was not going to get the ball if he didn't pick it up off of the ground.

Cherry and Dickie led Edmondson to two team titles in wrestling. Stanley won the 180-pound individual title both years. He was nicknamed "Don Eagle" after a professional wrestler of the '50s. Since Stanley was losing his hair on the sides, the name was even more appropriate.

○

Growing up, Wayne Jackson spent a lot of time in the Cherry household with Stanley and his three brothers. He became a "blood brother" and even slept in the same beds with Stanley and his siblings. Their mothers were also close friends.

Wayne attended Edmondson from 1965 to 1968. He lived in what was considered the low-grass area or the bottom of Edmondson Village. He used to play ball with neighborhood children at ABC Park, competing against other west Baltimore neighborhoods. The kids yearned for an indoor facility, so their parents got a petition signed by all the neighbors for a recreation center. Their strong community support was able to influence the Bureau of Recreation to eventually build Bentalou Recreation Center.

The "brothers" competed with one another, especially Wayne, Stanley, and Louis, and dreamed of being linebackers in the National Football League. Many afternoons the buddies would go to ABC Park and challenge any six guys to tackle football.

When Wayne first began high school, he did not try out for any sports. One afternoon, he was sitting on his front steps when a friend came by and asked, "Ain't you playing ball?" Wayne looked up, ran into his house, got some clothes, and went out for the football team. He weighed about 150 pounds then and was 5'9". After running over to Edmondson High, he was amazed to find the field covered with people. There were at least 200 players trying out for football.

Wayne made the junior varsity team as a second-string fullback, although he felt he was as good as the starting players. One day, the coach was frustrated and challenged the team. "Can anyone here run the football?" Wayne raised his hand, and from that point on, he started every game.

Edmondson was just beginning a football dynasty. Their '65 team won the MSA title. In 1966 they played City College for the championship and lost a close game. Stanley Cherry's brother Louis, who was a year ahead of Wayne, caught and ran the last pass of the game toward the end zone and almost scored a touchdown. Wayne was now playing varsity, and although he didn't start, he came in toward the end of the game and averaged ten yards per carry. Quarterback Kurt Schmoke, who also played lacrosse, led City. (Schmoke became the first elected black mayor of Baltimore.)

Coach Waibel left before Wayne's senior year to take the head football coaching job at Polytechnic High School (Poly). Former Douglass coach Charlie Robinson took over and led Edmondson to the MSA title. They even beat City that year, and Wayne was selected to the All-State team as a fullback.

The spring of Wayne's sophomore year he considered going out for baseball, the Jackson family sport. His father had been a great home run hitter in the old Negro League; and his brother was a semi-pro player. His dad and brother would throw balls for Wayne to hit in the alley behind their house. Wayne was not a good hitter but he was a great fielder. He played shortstop in the Harlem Park recreational league.

As Wayne walked through the gymnasium to the athletic fields, he saw a lot of students practicing lacrosse. His homeroom buddy, Johnny Magwood, urged Wayne to go out for the team, but if Wayne were going to play a sport that spring, it would be baseball. After watching some lacrosse practice through the fence, he walked over to the baseball field to get a closer look. Something about the lacrosse action excited him, so Wayne approached Coach Waibel and was put on the J.V. as a midfielder. His friend Johnny Magwood was an attackman, and they would throw the ball against the wall in Magwood's cellar after practice to better develop their skills.

Wayne and Johnny were very competitive, and would count up all of their goals and assists to see which one was the highest scorer. The competition made them both better players. It was always a game of one-upmanship.

There was a white lacrosse player named Rick Evans who was considered the coolest white dude at Edmondson High. Wayne and Magwood learned a lot about lacrosse technique from him. Unfortunately, Evans missed a lot of school, games, and practices. He was always AWOL, going on trips with his family. (Evans later made All-American in lacrosse at University of Baltimore.)

In Wayne's junior year, he tried out for varsity lacrosse and made the team. Against Friends School, a challenging private school competitor, Wayne was in the "zone"—he couldn't miss—and scored every goal in the game plus the overtime winning goal.

Before they played Friends School, the players had never seen the seriousness of the game of lacrosse from the preppy private school side. A large crowd of affluent people ringed the field. They saw families setting up lawn chairs to watch the game. This made the guys want to win in the worst way. Alonzo Chavis, a robust football lineman who played defense, had also fired the guys up by leading them in school fight songs on the bus.

Interestingly, Wayne never paid attention to news articles, television, statistics, or opposing great players. The only time he kept tabs on anything was against his friend, Johnny Magwood. Wayne always knew that he needed to score at least three goals in every game to keep up in his competition against Magwood.

Wayne recalled only one other opponent who got under his skin. During J.V. play, a strong, white Jewish boy named Gary Handleman from City College scored five goals off of Wayne. Wayne craved an opportunity for revenge. He did not want to be embarrassed like that ever again. After practices, he would go out to the park and have Stanley Cherry guard him while his dog chased after the shots. Wayne practiced shooting, dodging, and facing-off. He got to where he could even out-dodge the dog.

Early in Wayne's junior year, before the lacrosse season began, he attended a lacrosse clinic at Boys' Latin, a private school, at the urging of Coach Waibel. He was the only black there. He learned about caring for sticks; philosophies of offense and defense; and skills related to facing-off, learning the flip, and other "tricks of the trade."

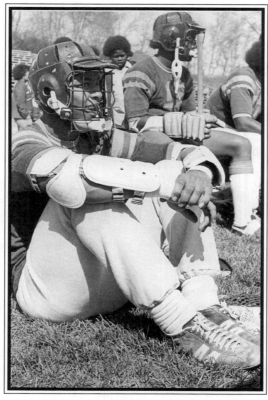

Midfielder Wayne Jackson. *(photo: Sid Brooks)*

In Wayne's senior year, Edmondson played City for the public school title. It was a chance for redemption against Handleman, and also City's goalie, Dominic Green, who lived around the corner from Wayne. The teams were tied at the end of regulation time. Wayne realized that whoever won the face-off in overtime between he and Handleman would be the game-maker. The opponents struggled for control of the ball from the middle of the field to behind City's goal where Wayne finally scooped it up and ran towards the goal. City stacked all of its defensemen in front of the goal, along with the goalie, minimizing the chance for any shots making it. Wayne began to fake and crank the ball, but couldn't shoot until he saw City's goalie rushing out towards him. Then he fired it over Green's shoulder for the winning goal.

Wayne also started in basketball his senior year, playing every position: center, forward, and guard.

○

Stanley Cherry was considered a bully, but in reality he loved to clown around. He just never knew when to stop. Wayne had a calming effect on him. In high school, Wayne and Stanley worked the night shift at the Trailways Bus Station washing dishes and cleaning the eatery. The best job "perk" was that Trailways allowed them to eat all they wanted, and this helped them bulk up for the football season.

Stanley felt he was as good as or better than Wayne in all sports, and kept trying to prove it. While Wayne was agile and a naturally gifted athlete, Cherry was bigger, more aggressive, and much stronger. With the exception of wrestling or boxing, every time they went one-on-one with each other in any sport, Wayne always dominated. Frustrated, Stanley would try to get the ball away from Wayne, whether it was in basketball, football, or lacrosse, but Wayne was always in control.

Wayne was playing football against Carver High in his last year at Edmondson and scored on an 85-yard run. The Carver coach was a friend of Earl Banks, and he told Wayne that he was very impressed and would contact him about possible recruitment. A few weeks later, the Carver coach and Banks went to Wayne's home to encourage him to attend Morgan State College.

Arizona State University and the University of Maryland also recruited Wayne. The brother of Arizona State's Dean of Students owned the gas station where Wayne worked part-time, and he sent his brother all of the sports articles about Wayne. The dean showed them to the Arizona State football coach and Wayne was offered a scholarship. The University of Maryland recruited Wayne for football and lacrosse. Even Johns Hopkins tried to recruit Wayne, but found out that he didn't qualify academically. Even though he had a "B" average, he was in a technical program, which automatically disqualified him for Hopkins.

One day Wayne even received a bus ticket by mail to travel to upstate New York to visit Army at West Point. Edmondson's principal, a military academy graduate, had recommended Wayne to Army's football coach. Wayne wanted to attend Army, but he never made use of the bus ticket. Unfortunately, there wasn't much guidance or advice in Wayne's home about college, so he just took care of himself. Wayne often stared at the West Point brochure and dreamt about Army. In the meantime, the guy who owned the gas station died, and Wayne never followed up on the Arizona State University offer.

So once again Wayne was sitting on his front steps. It was early August, he'd graduated from high school, and he didn't know what to do with his life. Woody Williams, the basketball coach at Lake Clifton High, drove by. "What are you doing, Wayne? Are you going to college?" Wayne told him no. "Get in the car," Williams ordered. He drove Wayne directly to Morgan and took him to Coach Banks' office. "Son, you're coming here," said Banks. "Be at practice tomorrow."

Although he wanted to play flanker or split end, Coach Banks put Wayne at fullback. The fullback position at Morgan blocked much more than he ran with the ball. Wayne found himself playing behind Joe Alex, but he did make the traveling team, an important accomplishment, since it meant going to New York to play against Grambling in the first Urban League contest before 65,000 fans at Yankee Stadium.

During the summer practice, Coach Banks liked Wayne's spunk at jumping to the front of the line to run the ball against the tough, mean Morgan defense. Wayne took off and ran a sweep against three future outstanding professional NFL players: Raymond Chester (Oakland Raiders), Mark Washington (Dallas Cowboys), and Willy Germany (Washington Redskins).

As a freshman, Wayne roomed with Joe Alex, the first white football player at Morgan. Joe was a graduate of Patterson High School where he was an All-State football and lacrosse player. He never complained and seldom ever discussed the fact that he was the only white player out there. At 6'4" and 240 pounds, he was a punishing fullback. He was the starter and Wayne was his backup. Joe was in his junior year when Wayne came in as a freshman. They were roommates on the road. Joe was basically a quiet guy, just sitting around smoking Marlboros.

Wayne dated Nikki, a young lady he met in high school at a neighborhood social function. His relationship with her was an open and respectful one. Since he was away a lot, they both dated other people, but still considered themselves a couple when he was back in Edmondson Village.

○

Up through the late '60s, Morgan State recruited very few in-state football players. Most of their team came from Texas and New Jersey. The only in-state players who were recruited came from City College, a high school that produced some excellent athletes who were also recruited by major colleges throughout the country. Occasionally, Morgan football alumni would recommend players from Douglass High, an all-black school, such as Ray Chester and Ben Eaton. But it was rare for players like Joe Alex from Patterson and Wayne Jackson of Edmondson to be recruited by Morgan State.

○

Morgan beat Grambling 9 to 7 that fall. It was the last time they would ever beat the great Grambling College teams. The next year, Wayne was in and out of school. He had a job at Western Electric for a naval weapons contract, but realized it was not the thing for him to do. He returned for the second semester after taking courses at the Community College of Baltimore so that he could participate in spring football.

○

Aside from Wayne, Hall, and Cherry, the initial Edmondson connection to Morgan State included Alonzo Chavis on defense, David Lewis in the goal, and Michael Mitchell on attack, a full 25 percent of the team. And the Edmondson alums were eagerly awaiting Morgan Holley, who had recently returned from Vietnam, in the spring. He was a fine defensive back in football and a very good lacrosse midfielder from Edmondson who joined the Marines after graduation.

○

I disliked Edmondson High from my own high school days. Traditionally, when a new school began athletics, they usually stunk for about five years. Recognizing this, school officials let the newly opened high schools play J.V. sports for the first two years.

So when my Forest Park High team played Edmondson's J.V. in my sophomore spring year of 1958, we figured on a big win. Not only did we lose to a "start-up" squad, the Edmondson players kicked us all over the field. On one play, Tom Bateman, a feared midfielder, came downfield on a fast break, knocking over one Forest Park defender and then running through and over me (breaking my stick) and scoring a goal. I was humiliated.

A year and a half later, Edmondson hosted Forest Park's football team in their first ever varsity game. On the kickoff, Bateman dislocated his shoulder and I, the fifth-string quarterback, envisioned an easy victory. Instead, Edmondson destroyed the Foresters 44 to 0.

○

I was coaching by the seat of my pants, and I knew it. Intrigued by the potential of my players, I worried I might shortchange them due to my lack of experience. So I decided to attend as many collegiate and club games as possible on the weekends to reacquaint myself with the strategy of lacrosse. I also got back in touch with many former teammates and opponents, some of whom offered various forms of assistance, including notes and handouts from clinics, books, and brief "guest coaching" visits to Morgan.

For example, Jerry Schnydman, a diminutive All-American from Johns Hopkins, played club ball with me, and played against me in high school and college. He was now Dean of Admissions at Hopkins and an assistant lacrosse coach. Schnydman, at barely 5'3" tall, was one of the greatest face-off specialists ever in lacrosse. He came out to Morgan on several occasions to work with Wayne, Poopie, and the rest of the midfielders.

I also enticed another former club teammate, Gene Fusting, one of the most prolific scorers of all time at both the college and club level, to work with the Morgan offense, especially the attackmen.

So, by the time the Ten Bears played their toughest opponent of the abbreviated 1970 season, the University of Maryland (UM) "B" team, both squad and coach had significantly improved.

The game, played on a UM practice field in College Park, was close. The Bears lost 12 to 9 but earned some hard-fought respect. The Maryland "B" team, dotted with several varsity players, had to play an outstanding game to hold on to victory despite a great game by the Bears' defense and goalie, David Lewis.

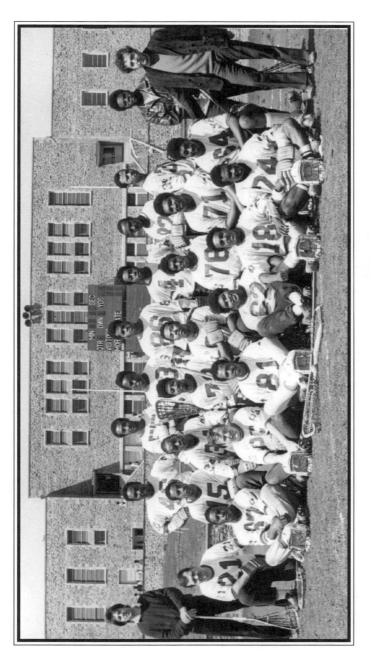

The 1970 Morgan State Lacrosse Club Team. *(photo: Sid Brooks)*

CHAPTER 4

RADICAL TIMES

SPRING 1970

Clarence "Tiger" Davis sat behind my desk in the graduate school office as I paced the floor. We were discussing the lacrosse team. Though Tiger wasn't on the team, he liked to keep on top of everything that was happening on campus—especially anything that impacted the college's social or political climate.

"We've got our first game against a regular college team," I said, referring to the upcoming contest against the University of Maryland Baltimore County (UMBC). "They're a good Division II squad. Up till now, we've only played community colleges, freshmen, and 'B' teams. It's important that we make a good showing."

"Good showing?" said Tiger as he rose to his feet. "This is a major struggle!"

"Struggle, my ass," I said. "It's a game; an athletic contest. And if we play well, maybe it'll convince the Athletic Department to let us go varsity next year."

Tiger walked over and hugged me. "My man," he said, "this team you've developed is about more than athletics. And don't you ever forget it. It's about race, the class system, politics, the sorry fabric of our society . . . Now, what courses should I take this summer?"

Davis was a student in Morgan's graduate school. Despite his activism and constant protests around the school, he had graduated on time.

Originally, he had thought about going on to law school. He would often speak to me in the graduate school office about his future. I advised him that a master's degree in history/social sciences might be more beneficial. So, Tiger enrolled in the graduate program and took classes from some of the great black thinkers of the time in history and social sciences, such as Ben Quarles, George Sinkler, David Lewis, and Parren Mitchell. Interestingly, his advisor was Tom Cripps, a white professor of Black History whom Tiger had constantly challenged as an undergraduate.

"Where ya going?" I asked as Tiger headed for the door.

"To lead a protest," he said.

"About what?" I continued to implore.

"I'm not sure, but the students are callin'."

The students all looked up to Tiger because he was their hero. He was the quintessential militant activist.

Through the window, I heard the students cheering as Tiger came out of Holmes Hall.

The issue was somewhat clouded but was basically against authority. It involved the firing and replacement of a faculty member by someone from Howard University, and the issue was that Morgan State was being made into a little elitist Howard University. So Tiger took the lead. He began:

pardon Martin Luther King
he was only dreaming
pardon brother Malcolm
he was only for real
pardon me, again, Mr. A merry ka
for truth is the light

○

Born in Wilkes County, Georgia in 1942, Tiger moved with his family to Baltimore in 1948. His father was having trouble with the Klan, an intimidating force in Georgia, at the sawmill where he worked. Tiger's dad had resisted giving money to Klansmen, and one night the Klan showed up to burn down the Davis home. However, the landowner, a white man, came out with a shotgun and screamed at the Klan, "You can't come on my land and tamper with my niggers!"

The Davis family moved to a Baltimore basement apartment. Tiger, his parents, brother, and one sister all lived in one room with a coal furnace, and were awakened every so often when the coal would come flying down the chute.

Tiger attended Dunbar Junior and Senior High Schools in east Baltimore, and he was the second-ranked academic student all the way through the eleventh grade. But, at the age of 16, he had a son out of wedlock and it affected his grades. He was captain of the football team and played four years of varsity. Among his teammates were quarterback Reginald Lewis, who later purchased Beatrice Foods, and Jim Norfleet, a split end who invented Ultrabrite toothpaste.

Segregated Dunbar began playing against white schools in 1956, but only in scrimmages. Then, in 1958, they were scheduled to play a regular game against Poly, which was the best team at that time in the public school division or MSA. The Dunbar football and basketball coach, "Sugar" Cain, was a tremendous motivator, as was Reginald Lewis. Both men spoke to the team about playing to the best of their abilities, not embarrassing the community, and winning the game. No one else believed they could come close. Dunbar won 12 to 8.

After graduating in 1960, instead of following his brother to college, Tiger decided to join the military. He was embarrassed that he had let his parents down by having a child with his girlfriend, Barbara. He enlisted in the U.S. Air Force with eight friends from Dunbar. They went in on the "buddy system."

Initially, Tiger was stationed at Lackland Air Force Base in San Antonio. Although he had experienced racism in Georgia and in Baltimore (his great-grandmother's cousin had been castrated by the Klan), he had never experienced it with white sidekicks. One night, Tiger and some Italian and Jewish guys he had befriended visited the strip joints in San Antonio where blacks were not allowed (even though the bawdy clubs were owned by former military officers). Not recognizing the reality of Southern racism as Tiger did, his white friends wanted to fight the doormen. Cooler heads prevailed.

Tiger had also experienced class racism in Baltimore among blacks because he was from the "country" and his skin color was much darker than others. In high school, Tiger majored in mathematics and Latin and was a top student. However, the award for finest student went to a girl he tutored because she was of lighter skin.

When Tiger returned from basic training in Texas, he had a second child, a daughter, with Barbara. His mom invited them to stay with her while Tiger was in the service.

For the next three and a half years, Tiger was stationed in England but traveled extensively. His assignments took him to Europe and temporary duty in Africa and Asia. It was the early '60s, and Tiger earned his *degree* in clandestine military history. He spent 15 days in Vietnam bringing in supplies in 1963. He knew it was to prepare for war. Military intelligence and the CIA were calling the shots. Tiger also served some time in the Congo, where the CIA was using its influence against Patrice Lumumba whom they feared would side with the Communists. And he observed similar activity in Libya against King Idris, who was later overthrown by Moammar Gadhafi.

While back in England, Tiger experienced the same segregation as in the States, especially in London and Liverpool. He and his black Air Force comrades discovered they were only allowed to associate with certain groups; so Tiger and the guys hung out with Africans and Jamaicans.

Tiger decided to give up his military career and return to the States to be with his family, which had grown to three children. He wanted a college education and to regain his parents' trust. So in 1964, he returned to the U.S., enrolled at Morgan State College, and began working full-time at Bethlehem Steel.

One day, Tiger approached his mom. "I want to marry Barbara."

She paused. "Now you're old enough to make that decision. You weren't old enough when you were sixteen."

Tiger ran to his father and got his approval. He took an extra day off from Bethlehem Steel and moved to the Kennedy Apartments in Baltimore in the summer of 1965. His kids were then two, five, and six years old. He chose to get married on the same day his parents celebrated their wedding anniversary.

Tiger actually got out of the Air Force a few weeks before his official tour of duty was up because his granddad had died. The death had an aura of suspected foul play. His granddad was getting off of a train in South Carolina shortly before he was found dead. No one ever knew why or what happened.

Disturbed over the events, Tiger returned from the funeral and met up with some friends around Morgan State. They went to a party with a lot of the guys from his graduating class at Dunbar. On the way back from the party, they got into a car accident with an elderly white man.

An ambulance arrived and took a bleeding Tiger and the old man to Union Memorial Hospital in north Baltimore City. As Tiger was wheeled in, the nurse brusquely asked, "What's wrong with you, boy?"

Tiger responded, "Uncle Sam ain't got no boys, bitch, only men." It was a reflexive response that he had given time and time again while in the service.

The nurse became hysterical. She summoned the ambulance drivers, who knocked Tiger out of the wheelchair and started choking him. A fight evolved in the emergency room as the combatants rolled all over the floor. The cops were called in. They put Tiger in chains, beat him up, and took him to the City Jail.

Tiger called his dad at five a.m. "I need $105 to get bailed out."

A month later, when they went to court, the judge asked Tiger, "Why didn't you just go to Provident Hospital?" Provident was a black hospital.

"Why should I go there?" asked Tiger incredulously. "I'm an American GI. I can go to white Union Memorial Hospital if I want to. Why should I have to go to a black one?"

The judge placed Tiger on probation.

Tiger was incensed. He went out and joined the Congress On Racial Equality (C.O.R.E.). He became a civil rights worker-trainee. There he learned how to deal with abuse without fighting back. They'd provoke each other in ways such as mashing eggs on each other's heads. It was like being a pledge in a college fraternity. This was difficult for Tiger; he wanted to fight back. So he left for a while. Eventually, he rejoined C.O.R.E. in their civil rights marches in the South.

Tiger was turned off during one of the C.O.R.E. marches in Selma because he could not believe the protesters wouldn't fight back. He liked being together with whites during civil rights marches, but he could not accept the pacifist ideology of Martin Luther King or C.O.R.E. So he drifted to the ideology of Black Power and adopted it. That's when Tiger really found his calling. He related to how other minorities in the country used their power and economic impact.

Death meant nothing to Tiger. His brothers were coming home in body bags from Vietnam. He and his friends began to arm themselves.

His mom was upset. "What's all this talk about burning and looting with Black Power?" she asked. "And go get a haircut!"

At Morgan State, Tiger joined the fraternity Groove Phi Groove, a social fellowship made up of a lot of athletes and Vietnam veterans.

Tiger wore sunglasses with the other vets in class. They all had large Afros and smoked marijuana.

○

Trouble was everywhere on the campus of Morgan State in the late '60s. In March of '68, black students were against anything white. As a matter of fact, Tiger Davis wouldn't even shake the hand of Dr. Cripps, a white professor who taught Black History. A returning veteran from the Air Force, Tiger was a recognized leader on campus, and, although an undergraduate, he was older and wiser than most of his classmates.

The student body protested everything: lack of Black Studies Programs, mandatory ROTC, coed dorms, curfew issues, and so on. Male students became politicized over the concern that the nine p.m. curfew in women's dorms was basically blocking access to the "sisters." Coed dorms would give the guys a better shot at the women. With Tiger in the lead, the students won each of these protest issues. They were even able to receive college credit for working in the community, and participating in protests was considered part of that work.

Martin Jenkins, President of Morgan, couldn't overtly propose many of these controversial issues, but he did encourage them clandestinely. Holding on to archaic rules for the sake of tradition was not his style. While he refused to negotiate openly with the protesting students, Jenkins was still able to manipulate them to capitulate publicly to support the president. In the end, the students still won all of their demands. This give-and-take was a showing of respect for elders, which was important to Tiger Davis. President Jenkins understood the student psyche and was able to accomplish what other historically black campus presidents could not. While he was always quoted as saying he would only deal with the Student Government Association, he knew the common-sense approach was to deal with all of the students and protesters.

President Jenkins gave all of the disciplinary power to the students through the Student Court, and in the mid-sixties Tiger served as Chief Justice. During this time, there was a very promiscuous young lady whom the dorm mother wanted removed from the school. However, several members of the Student Court had had sex with this woman and were reluctant to see her expelled. Eventually, they suspended her for the remainder of the semester, and then let her reenroll for the next term.

Tiger was now commuting from Harford County, approximately 35 miles from Morgan, after he helped the locals secure a community development grant. He became their executive director and carried out the mission of the community to build housing and recreation, and to structure an avocation program. These were all strategies to help overcome poverty. As a result of his community activism, the Public Broadcasting Station decided to hire Tiger to do a weekly show called *Strategy for Action*. The producer wanted Tiger to attack guests for their opinions. It ran for two years.

However, during a racial incident on Maryland's Eastern Shore, Tiger was out on the streets shouting, "If a hair on anyone black is injured, we will burn this town down!" Someone alerted the management at Public Broadcasting, and, although he had been there for two years, Tiger was advised that he had to audition again for the show. Following the audition, he was told that he didn't have the qualifications to be the show's host.

○

Tiger's assertion that the Bears' match against UMBC was a major struggle proved to be right on the mark. UMBC was on the verge of becoming a top-ten NCAA Division II lacrosse team when they played the Bears, and it was the beginning of a bitter rivalry. The UMBC players were skilled at every position and extremely well coached by the feisty Dick Watts. It was obvious that he had scouted the Bears and knew all of their strengths and weaknesses.

The game was played well defensively except in unsettled situations (broken plays or fast breaks), and therein laid our downfall. The massive footballers were intimidating and the UMBC contest was a brutal event. With Stan Cherry, Bruce Caraway, and Harold Bell leading the charge, the bodychecking, hitting, and contact shook the grounds of UMBC's home field in Catonsville, Maryland. (Each of them would be selected to a football All-American team.)

Like other schools, UMBC double- and triple-teamed Wayne Jackson, the key to the Bears' offense. They also tried cutting off Miles Harrison Jr. and Ben Kimbers and forced Morgan into having less skilled players control the ball. Although Wayne and the others scored, it was not enough.

The Bears played perhaps their finest game of the season, but UMBC prevailed 12 to 8.

○

Against UMBC, Miles Harrison Jr. scores on his patented jumpshot. *(photo: the* Baltimore News American, *Charles Hart)*

Maybe Tiger was right—maybe there were parallels between our fledgling lacrosse team and the overall black struggle for equality and racial justice.

As Tiger was rallying the students over various race issues, I was campaigning to have the team go varsity. At the varsity level, we could truly compete and make a name for ourselves.

I wasn't only thinking of potential victories or championships, but also of what excelling at the sport of lacrosse could do for these players.

Lacrosse might be called the ultimate contact sport—off the field.

There were an amazing number of successful business and professional men in the Baltimore area with lacrosse in their backgrounds. It just may have been the springboard that launched their careers.

In the '40s, those who were very proficient at the game of lacrosse were almost all "born with a silver stick in their mouths." At that time, it was a "rich boys" sport and an elitist game.

It carried over into the business world from father to son. These were people who had money, and, as a result, a lot of things were inherited—not just the prep school admissions, but also entrée into certain circles outside of school and sport.

Lacrosse is like membership in a select fraternity. In no other sport are coaches and players such good friends off the field. And, as a result of this phenomenon, social clubs have been built around the sport. Suddenly, the lacrosse player finds himself going to "lacrosse" bars and "lacrosse" bull roasts, and a part of an extensive "lacrosse" fraternity.

Many of the most prestigious universities have lacrosse as a major sport, producing smart kids with lacrosse backgrounds. Consequently, a lot of kids from lacrosse went into specialized professions such as law and medicine.

Lacrosse was polo without horses—an upper-class sport. At the other end of the spectrum was soccer, a working-class sport. For example, at Loyola College there was always jealousy between former prep lacrosse players and soccer players from public schools. Lacrosse was part of the preppy roots. It went back a lot of generations, and was a very narrow world. With lacrosse, that world came down to a lot of conservative business people.

Baltimore became the center for club lacrosse. As players moved from their college days into club lacrosse, they gravitated toward other people from influential backgrounds who also moved on into their fathers' businesses, professions, and so on. Contacts were made through lacrosse, similar to those associated with football players in the South.

When businessmen who were very enthusiastic about a sport met other young players, they saw more than just sports potential in that individual. People in business tried to hire athletes because the team cooperation, stamina, and competition required in lacrosse seemed to translate well in the business world.

Lacrosse was the only team game that was not professional. No one profited from lacrosse, and it was not a big money sport. Other "genteel" sports such as tennis and golf went professional, and it had a dramatic effect on the sports—sometimes for the worse.

Although intensely played, lacrosse was played for fun and competition, leaving plenty of room for camaraderie. Lacrosse requires a good team attitude as is crucial in business. But some people saw this lacrosse "network" as slightly more conspiratorial.

Some looked at the "Gilman Connection." The connection began at Calvert Prep School in north Baltimore where a kid went from the first to the sixth grade. From there he matriculated to Gilman, an expensive, selective, preppy private high school. Then most of these young men moved on to Princeton or another Ivy League school.

There were an awful lot of Princeton and Ivy League lacrosse All-Americans who worked for major law firms and banks in the Baltimore area. Lacrosse was the calling card, an uptown sport. Contacts made on the field evolved into long-term business and social relationships. Boys with sticks developed into men with briefcases.

Lacrosse was in the public eye in Baltimore, and businesses wanted to benefit from that. So, a kind of unspoken brotherhood existed in the Baltimore area. The list of successful people who belonged was impressive. What had evolved could be explained as a form of corporate genetics, with a preselection process where the odds were good that someone with a top education who had demonstrated leadership in sports, such as lacrosse, was viewed as a highly viable business commodity. Lacrosse had made such people highly visible. And the social life that accompanied the sport kept them visible long after they'd finished playing.

○

It was this lacrosse world that Schnoo Snyder and I loved and were peripherally a part of. While neither of us had come from a rich Gentile background, gone to a private school, nor played lacrosse before we were 14 years old, we had played the game and been bitten by it. By playing with and against the private school elite, and then socializing amongst them, we gained entrée into the lacrosse brotherhood.

Schnoo gained it as an All-State high school and collegiate All-American defenseman—feared and respected. And his sarcastic personality and quick wit endeared him to many followers of the game.

Again, I was a fair player on my best day, and my high school and college teams went from mostly poor to one above-average season. However, the year I was ineligible (when transferring from Maryland to the University of Baltimore), I played for the University Club lacrosse team. That team, in 1963, won the U.S. Open Lacrosse Championship. Not only did I become friendly with many of the players who would go on to be head coaches of great collegiate teams of the '70s, but I gained a top-level education in lacrosse technique and strategy. And by being a member of a once-in-a-lifetime "dream team," I achieved instant credibility in the extended lacrosse family.

That spring of '70 as Schnoo and I hurried into the clubhouse entrance of Pimlico Race Track, we discussed my venture at Morgan.

"If I can get the school to go varsity next year," I explained, "we could surprise a lot of teams, and the whole lacrosse scene."

Schnoo hadn't seen this much enthusiasm from me in years.

"You can't be serious," he said. "True, you've got a few great athletes, some with decent lacrosse skills, but, no way."

I smiled. I had expected this.

"Why can't Morgan succeed?" I asked.

"Because," said Schnoo, studying the *Racing Form* for the first race, "your players have little experience, there's no feeder system, lacrosse is foreign to most of them, and Morgan will never give you the financial and moral support that you need."

I digested his remarks and waited until Schnoo bet the race and saw it to its conclusion. It was useless to try to engage Schnoo's attention while a race was in progress.

"You forget," I countered, "that black kids have been playing in the city for the better part of the '60s, and some have played extremely well. That will continue—so there is a feeder system. The same holds true for blacks in some New Jersey and Long Island schools. Also, *we* never played till high school—most of the guys on your great City College team only began playing, at best, in the ninth grade. As for Morgan State's support, you may be right. I'll just have to wait and see."

I followed Schnoo to the paddock to view the horses for the next race.

"Lacrosse is still foreign to your players, as a sport and culturally," said Schnoo. "You don't have a philosophy or strategy of where you're going . . . Maybe, you'll win two to four games a year, but that's the extent of it. Yeah, I know there are exceptions, like Jim Brown and some other blacks who played in the Ivy League and at the military academies, but they are anomalies."

From the paddock, we walked outside to the grandstands and felt the cool spring breeze of the sunny day.

"I do have a philosophy," I argued. "I'm gonna follow exactly what Coach Bilderback did at Navy when he won all those NCAA Championships, and beat your Maryland team consistently. He recruited two or three good lacrosse players and surrounded them with great athletes and football players to whom he stressed the fundamentals of the game. The cultural part will take a while, but I'll bet my kids come to love the game. Lacrosse can gain them entrée into a new world. It'll get them social contacts, jobs, you name it."

Schnoo began laughing and almost lost his place in the *Racing Form*. "I hate to burst your bubble," he said, "but you're dreaming. No black college can just begin playing and expect to win or be accepted by the blue bloods. It'll never, ever happen!"

○

A Morgan State student, Irving H. "Ochiki" Young, was among 31 Black Panthers and sympathizers arrested for the murder of an informant. Somehow the police saw him as their prime suspect. He was among 12 who were later indicted.

Tiger Davis, although not a member of the Black Panther party, saw himself as a Pan-African revolutionary. A strong supporter and advocate of the black struggle, he held a rally at the Panther's Free Medical Clinic on Greenmount Avenue and raised thousands of dollars in one evening.

"I need your support," he yelled to the crowd, "but first I need your checkbooks."

The crowd was made up of white Johns Hopkins students and liberals from the surrounding Charles Village neighborhood.

Eventually, Ochiki Young was the only one convicted and sent to jail. A national rally evolved around him called the *Free Ochiki Movement*.

○

The Bears had beaten Essex Community College 9 to 2 and were preparing for their final encounter of the season, the varsity Division II team, Mount St. Mary's, from Emmitsburg, Maryland. Although not on the same level as UMBC, they had an experienced lacrosse program.

The practice was spirited and I was pleased. Suddenly, Cherry, Poopie, and a couple of other players stopped practicing and ran over to me.

"Don't be obvious," Poopie said, "but look over behind the goalpost. There's a guy who's been taking pictures of us for the past two days. We're gonna fake like we're jogging around the track and jump him and get the camera."

"These are troubled times," whispered Cherry. "Maybe you don't get it because you're white, but there's a struggle going on. The CIA, FBI, state police, and city cops have infiltrated lots of groups. He's probably with the cops."

"Yeah," said Poopie, "I can dig it."

Poopie's response to everything was "I can dig it," and everyone had picked it up. (I began using the phrase at home and at work, always drawing raised eyebrows.)

Just then, Miles Harrison Jr. came running over.

"Why'd we stop practicing? What's going on?" he asked.

"Stanley and Poopie believe that the photographer behind the goalpost is spying on the team, trying to infiltrate us because we are really a revolutionary group looking to overthrow . . . Who are we looking to overthrow, Poopie?" I asked sarcastically.

"Hold on," said Miles. "He's a friend of mine named DeWayne Wickham, and he's a photojournalist. Hell, Poopie, he's like you— a returning Vietnam vet who's enrolled at Morgan. By the way, he's got great photos of the war."

"So what's he want?" asked Cherry.

"Nothing." answered Miles. "He's only taking photos of the sport of lacrosse. Maybe he'll give us some."

The players renewed practice, and Cherry and Poopie were especially aggressive and seemed to be preening for the photographer the rest of the afternoon.

A week later, DeWayne stopped by and gave me dozens of great photos of the Bears in action.

O

Towards the end of our maiden lacrosse season, I was still second-guessing my coaching acumen. This led me to seek the dean's advice.

Gingerly, I approached Dr. DeCosta, who had recently returned from conducting research on his book for the Carnegie Foundation.

"Dean," I said, "there's something I need to discuss with you. It's about this lacrosse team I'm coaching."

The dean leaned back in his chair behind his desk and motioned for me to take a seat.

"Silverman," he began, "you remember that when I hired you I was emphatic that whatever hours you worked, it was imperative that you be here between the hours of six p.m. and ten p.m. while the graduate school is in session. Now I hope you are not looking to change that. Especially while I'm on this sabbatical."

"No, Dean," I said, "it's nothing like that. Although if it happens that we have an away game and I can't get back . . ."

"Hold on," ordered the dean. "You've got to make sure you're here. If something comes up or there's an emergency, you must make arrangements in advance. I can't be here, and we need someone to answer questions the students may have during the evening."

The graduate school courses were held mainly in the evening, except for the math and science programs. It was important for administrative and advisory support to be available until the students had completed their classes and left the campus.

"Oh, it's not about that, Dean," I said, "and, of course, I'll be here. Don't even give it a second thought. My concern is, though, about coaching the lacrosse team. I'm kind of a rookie, and not real sure how to teach the game and impart my lacrosse experience to a lot of players who never played it; or might not have received the correct coaching at the high school level, and . . ."

"Silverman," interrupted the dean, "let me tell you what I know about coaching. It's like running any kind of organization. The easiest part is showing the players what to do once they're on the field. Getting them to the field, though, is another matter. Coaching is all about planning, organization, and psychology, and I include motivation there. Those are the difficult parts. That's 70 to 80 percent of the game, and what differentiates the winners from the losers. Always remember that. The easiest part is what's left once you have them on the field. The toughest part is getting them to the field and keeping them there."

○

It was the last game of the season. Morgan State versus Mount St. Mary's. An experienced team, Mount St. Mary's was being dominated by the Ten Bears. To hold the scoring down, I had "benched" Dickie Hall and Wayne for the second half. Hall was incensed.

A couple of fights broke out. The same Morgan player, Blaine White, was involved in each fracas. When the last fight was broken up, I asked Blaine, "What's going on?"

"That guy kept calling me white," explained Blaine, "and I don't like anything white."

"But, your last name's White," I said.

"Doesn't matter," said Blaine as he ran back onto the field.

Later, Blaine got hurt in a pileup and there was no medical help. I told him to wait by his car and we'd go to see Larry Becker, a surgeon friend.

"Jesus," exclaimed Blaine sarcastically. "This isn't what Morgan does for injured players, Chip. You're just supposed to leave me here and forget about it!"

Blaine White had arrived at Morgan State two years earlier. At 6'6" and weighing 230 pounds, Blaine strutted around with his high school football jacket from MSA champion Poly with its large chenille football letters. At the beginning of football practice, the team took a jog around the field. Blaine ran awkwardly and some-how fell into a hole and broke his leg. When the players told Coach Banks what happened, he said, "Just let him lay there. He'll never be a Morgan football player the way he runs." (Actually, Blaine made the football team as a defensive lineman.)

Morgan defeated Mount St. Mary's 13 to 4 and completed its first season with five wins and three losses.

O

I asked the dean how much of a raise I would get during the next budget cycle. My wedding was in two months, and I was con-cerned about how to support a family on my present salary.

"After I got my Ph.D. in Education from the University of Pennsylvania in the '30s," said the Dean, "I was appointed princi-

Attackman Dickie Hall scoring a goal against Mount St. Mary's.
(photo: DeWayne Wickham)

pal at Alabama Normal School. My salary was $3,600 a year. You should not get your hopes up too high. The president doesn't approve large raises."

"But, Dean," I pleaded, "this isn't 1936. It's over 30 years later. How am I going to live?"

"Patience," said the dean to me. "You must understand it takes time, and time is patience."

President Jenkins and Dr. DeCosta did not want me to leave Morgan. To them, I was a good teacher and administrator solidly entrenched in historic black Morgan State. I was involved, not just in administration, but in teaching on the graduate and undergraduate level, and in coaching the lacrosse team. Eventually, I could become one of the first white deans of a black college, after Dr. DeCosta retired in a few years.

I recognized that I could not live off of my current salary and, after much deliberation, had decided to work for the State Drug Abuse Administration, which came under the Maryland State Department of Health and Mental Hygiene. President Jenkins got wind of my plan to leave Morgan State and called Governor Mandel, telling him to intervene and keep me at Morgan.

The Assistant Secretary of Health, who had offered me the job, called and informed me that there was a tremendous amount of pressure coming from Morgan State via the Governor's Office, and it appeared that I wouldn't get the job. I was extremely agitated. Sprinting over to the Administration Building from my office in Holmes Hall, I barged in on President Jenkins.

"What are you trying to do to me?" I screamed. "This is slavery. You can't keep me here against my will!"

President Jenkins smiled, never getting up from his desk, and ordered me to sit down.

"Silverman," he said, "we think you're an important cog here at Morgan, and we'd like for you to stay. And, if I have to use my influence to keep you here, I will. I think it's a good career move, whether you recognize it or not."

I leaped up from my chair. "Let me tell you something. I'll quit right now. As a matter of fact, I quit. You can't force me to stay. I won't tolerate it. I'm leaving Morgan State. And I don't care if I don't work for the State Health Department or the Drug Abuse Administration. It doesn't matter. I'll get a job somewhere else. I can't believe you would do this to me."

"Sit still and calm yourself down," said President Jenkins. "What is it you want?"

I regained my composure and sat for a while watching the president. "Money. I want more money. You've got it in the budget to give me $9,800, but the dean had promised me more. He told me that you had cut the budget."

Jenkins smiled. "That's not exactly right. I can give you as much as $10,500, but that's the limit. What do you say?"

"President Jenkins," I said, smiling back, "I can start at 15 grand for the State Health Department. That's a lot more than $10,500."

"But, Chip, I guarantee you, you'll be dean of the graduate school one day."

"Yeah," I said. "I can just see it. Dean DeCosta will be here for years. He'll live forever. I won't get the job for 20 more years. There's no question about it. He's in excellent condition . . ."

"Yes, I know," said Jenkins. "Even though he just had a pacemaker put in his heart, he's in great shape. He was a great athlete, never gets stressed, and I've never seen him upset. He might just live forever."

"I can't wait," I said.

Jenkins rose slowly from his desk and looked out the window at Hillen Road.

"I can't pay you $15,000," he said. "I can't come close to it. Ten thousand five hundred dollars, that's it. I never go over budget. That's all your job is worth right now. If you insist on leaving, I won't stop you. But you're going to have to compromise."

"What do you mean?" I asked.

Jenkins explained that he wanted me to stay on until the end of the summer of 1970.

"I would like to see you remain as lacrosse coach, and teach graduate and undergraduate courses. Mainly, I'd appreciate a smooth transition so that when Dr. DeCosta comes back from his sabbatical, the graduation of students will be completed. And, the catalog and classes for the fall semester would be done, and the summer graduate school would be concluded."

I remained seated, thinking for a while, gazing upon the walls of the president's office covered with degrees and citations. I thought about the team and the players I'd be letting down if I walked out of there without looking back. They'd come a long way, but I truly believed I could help them go even further.

"Okay, President Jenkins. You've treated me great here except for the first 20 minutes of this conversation. I'll do all you ask, and I'll coach lacrosse—if the program goes varsity."

As I stood up to leave, President Jenkins said, "I don't think you'll have a lot of trouble with the Athletic Department agreeing to that. And I'll personally call Governor Mandel and make sure you still have your job at the Health Department at the end of the summer."

○

Although Marvin Mandel was not officially elected until 1970, he had served as governor of Maryland for about two years. As Speaker of the House of Delegates, he was next in line when the current governor, Spiro T. Agnew, was tapped as the vice-presidential nominee for Richard Nixon in the 1968 election.

Following the winning campaign of the Nixon-Agnew ticket, Mandel became governor.

Agnew, a relatively unknown Republican politician, had meteorically risen from PTA president to county executive of Baltimore County to governor of Maryland.

Dr. DeCosta's son, Frank Jr., became Agnew's chief advisor in Maryland, and, later, his deputy or legal advisor when he ascended to the vice presidency.

Perceived as the archconservative of the seventies, very few were aware that one of Agnew's key confidants was black.

Agnew graduated from Forest Park High School in the late thirties; the same high school that graduated me in the late fifties and Miles Harrison Jr. in the late sixties. Interestingly, Forest Park graduated numerous celebrities from the entertainment business, such as movie director and screenwriter Barry Levinson; Mama Cass Elliot (formerly Ellen Cohen); Ken Waissman and Maxine Fox, who produced *Grease* (the Broadway play loosely based on their times at Forest Park); and Otis Dammon Harris, who sang with *The Temptations*.

○

While strolling across campus by Holmes Hall, I saw Earl Banks, who asked if I was coming back next year to coach.

"I'm not sure," I said. "I have an offer at the State Drug Abuse Administration."

"What will it take to get you back?" asked Banks.

"If the team could go varsity, I'd reconsider."

Coach Banks was perspiring in the summer heat and wiping his neck with his handkerchief. "Well, how do we do that, Sibman?"

(Banks' hurried pronunciation of my last name.)

"We'd have to register with the United States Intercollegiate Lacrosse Association and that's only $1,500," I said, shifting from one foot to the other.

"Well, if that's what it takes, okay," said Banks. "As long as you come back and coach these kids, it'll take the heat off of me with the academic side. Since you'll be playing all-white schools, which no black colleges have ever done before, the faculty and administration will love it."

I was elated and smiled. "Are you surprised that we were pretty successful as a club team?"

"Well, hell no!" exclaimed Banks becoming very animated. "If you were one of them preppy white lacrosse kids and you saw ten niggers with sticks coming at you, you'd be scared shitless,

Athletic Director and Football Coach Earl "Papa Bear" Banks. *(photo: Promethean 1975, Morgan State College Yearbook)*

too! Of course I'm not surprised."

Earl Banks was considered one of the greatest coaches of collegiate football in the U.S. "Papa Bear's" accomplishments were truly awesome. In only a dozen years, his Morgan teams had twice led the nation in total defense, posted an incredible .850 winning percentage, a thirty-one-game winning streak, three unbeaten seasons, five CIAA (Central Intercollegiate Athletic Association) Championships, and gone to four bowl games. Plus, he had sent dozens of Hall-of-Fame-caliber players to the NFL.

○

That summer, I sadly left my graduate school position and the dean, Dr. DeCosta, to work for the Maryland State Drug Abuse Administration.

While my management skills would not be sorely missed, another Morgan administrator's would—President Martin Jenkins. After 22 years, he put in his surprise resignation to become Director

Dr. Martin Jenkins, President of Morgan State College. *(photo:* Promethean 1975, *Morgan State College Yearbook)*

of the Urban Affairs Office of the American Council on Education.

Born in Terre Haute, Indiana, Dr. Jenkins was educated at Howard University (A.B., 1925), Indiana State University (A.B., 1930), and Northwestern University (M.S., 1933 and Ph.D., 1935). Before becoming President of Morgan State College, he was Professor of Education at Howard University, Senior Specialist in Higher Education at the U.S. Office of Education, Dean of Instruction at Cheyney State Teachers College, Registrar and Professor of Education at North Carolina A. & T. College, and Instructor of Education at Virginia State College.

A distinguished American educator, Martin Jenkins wrote and lectured on many subjects, especially those concerning the gifted child, racial differences, and higher education. He participated in various surveys and studies in 20 or more states. Under the auspices of the U.S. Department of State, he lectured on educational topics at institutions in France, Norway, Sweden, Greece, Italy, and Lebanon.

Jenkins was published in more than 80 books, monographs, and periodicals. A member of Phi Beta Kappa, Dr. Jenkins was the recipient of eight honorary degrees and numerous commendations and citations for civic, educational, and community activities.

○

The H. Rap Brown trial moved from Bel Air, Maryland to Ellicott City in Howard County due again to pre-trial publicity.

Rap Brown failed to appear at his trial and an arrest warrant was issued for unlawful flight. A couple of days later, the FBI added Brown to an expanded Ten Most Wanted List (as number eleven).

Tiger was visiting my office and discussing a rally on the campus.

"See those brothers—urging the students to burn down the school?" he said. "They're agent provocateurs."

"What do you mean?" I asked.

"The ones who encourage killing and burning are agents, informants. We'd never advocate burning Morgan State."

"So," I asked, "the police infiltrate a couple of these radical groups with one or two informants?"

"No, you fool," laughed Tiger. "There are more agents out there than activists, workers, or revolutionaries put together!"

"Where's Rap Brown?" I asked.

"Probably New York or Baton Rouge where he's from," answered Tiger. "Nobody knows for sure. They're afraid the police will find out and try to kill him."

CHAPTER 5

LACROSSE'S ORIGINAL "WHITE SHADOW"

FALL 1970

The Other-Race Grant was originally designed for black students to attend white colleges. Later it served as an enticement to integrate historically black colleges. I used the Other-Race Grant to recruit white players who excelled in lacrosse; only I told them it was a lacrosse scholarship.

At Northern High School, near Morgan, I was recruiting a short white kid, Courtenay Servary, who played midfield and goalie, and a black player named George Kelly.

During the late summer and early fall, I contacted various freshmen who arrived at Morgan with lacrosse experience. One was a white Jewish student from my mother's neighborhood named Andi Arenson.

Andi grew up in an elegant home in northwest Baltimore City. His parents were fairly well-off, and, like many of the Jewish middle and upper class, they were politically very liberal. Their views were socialist and some people referred to them as extreme. Andi's father was a Southern Jew, while his mom came from Baltimore Jewish aristocracy.

In the mid-sixties, his parents separated, and Andi almost had a nervous breakdown. Divorce at that time was not as common as today and looked down upon. That, combined with moving with his mother to a small row house and her having to work (the family's financial reserves had dried up), made Andi a pariah in the eyes of most of his boyhood friends.

While most of Andi's old buddies went off to high school in Baltimore County or to private institutions, he attended Northwestern High, the majority black public school up the street. Andi escaped his woes at home by submerging himself in athletics and radical politics, and protests. He developed a close affinity to his black classmates.

In his senior year, Andi applied to numerous colleges hoping for an academic or athletic scholarship. But, even though he was a bright student and able athlete, all of his applications were rejected. Later, he discovered that his high school administration had sent adverse recommendations due to his openly radical leanings.

Despondent, he approached a black guidance counselor who explained the Other-Race Grant to Andi and encouraged him to consider it. Andi decided to go to Morgan State College. The Other-Race Grant included room and board and expenses for travel and incidentals.

Very rarely did the white students choose to live on campus at Morgan; and for those who did, the average length of time they roomed in the dorms was about 30 minutes.

Andi arrived at Morgan, was assigned to a new and modern dormitory, but opted for one of the older units. He fantasized about meeting the ghosts of radicals past or of the Underground Railroad from Civil War days.

Reality hit Andi as he carried a stereo into his dorm room. Everything was in disarray, and his roommate was sprawled partly on the bed and partly on the floor. Andi noticed an abundance of tarnished and charred spoons on the desk. Naively, he asked, "Do you collect antique spoons?" No response. Again, naively, Andi ventured, "Do you play the spoons?"

"Listen, you dumb fuckin' honky," began the roommate, "I cooks my dope in 'em. Now, give me 20 bucks!"

Andi put the stereo down and excused himself to go to the toilet. He went into the communal restroom and shower and realized that there were no doors or walls on the three stalls. They'd been removed. The only empty toilet seat was in the middle of two Nigerian exchange students who were having a discussion in their native tongue. Suddenly, Andi lost the desire to defecate, and maybe even to matriculate.

He returned to the dorm room to find the stereo and his roommate missing. Hustling down the steps, Andi jumped into his mother's car and drove back home. His life as an on-campus resident at Morgan had lasted less than 20 minutes. Andi would commute for the next four years.

It was several weeks before Andi found out that the individual he thought was his roommate was not even a student, but a junkie who had snuck into the dorm room the night before.

WINTER 1970-71

The beginning of the school year brought new additions to our team, renewed friendships among returning students, and a new challenge for myself. I was now Deputy Director of the Maryland State Drug Abuse Administration; and also married. Despite my new responsibilities, I remained committed to the team and had faith that they would one day be competing at an exceptionally high level of play. And I planned to be there when that happened.

That winter, I attended my first U.S. Intercollegiate Lacrosse Association Conference in Philadelphia. I scheduled games for Morgan's initial varsity season. It proved easy. Teams couldn't wait to play Morgan's new and inexperienced team, figuring that blacks wouldn't know how to play the game, thus adding a sure win to their schedules.

Peter Good, the British lacrosse and soccer coach at Amherst, readily agreed to schedule a match, assuming he'd be getting an easy game. There was only one coach I approached at the conference who would not play Morgan because it was a black school. Amazingly, it was the College of William and Mary, a top Southern academic institution known for its liberal leanings; and like me, its coach was Jewish.

O

I was proud of the lacrosse team and supported them in their other academic and athletic endeavors. I had great respect for the players, many of whom had overcome enormous obstacles just to survive childhood and make it to college. It saddened me to learn that some of them still had an inherent distrust of whites, including me, which made them question my character.

One winter afternoon, Poopie was working out, running around campus with his stick and throwing the ball against any dorm or classroom wall he came upon. He was joined by Morgan Holley, another Vietnam vet and former Edmondson player. Students and faculty were watching the guys and shaking their heads in wonder.

Later, Poopie ran into the gym where Cherry was wrestling, and they got into a discussion. Cherry told Poopie that he had recently won the Black College Wrestling Championship and was invited to the NCAAs (the National College Tournament). However, Morgan's Athletic Department would not pay the entry fee for him to compete in the National Championships in Kansas.

Poopie called me, and I, in turn, told Cherry that I would pay the $250 fee. Cherry refused the offer. In a subsequent phone conversation with Poopie, Cherry explained sadly, "Chip is white and must have an ulterior motive."

SPRING 1971

The Maryland Drug Abuse Administration was located about 20 minutes from Morgan. I worked from eight-thirty to four-thirty.

Because of my new schedule, I couldn't be at the beginning of practices all the time. Fortunately, I had Schnoo Snyder to fill in on occasion. Unfortunately, Schnoo preferred the racetrack at Pimlico to coaching the players. And missing even one race put Schnoo in a bad mood. Therefore, while waiting for me, Schnoo would act Vince-Lombardi-like, no nonsense and dictatorial, and the players grew to dislike him due to his attitude.

In many games, I was called upon by the referees to keep the official scorebook and be the timekeeper. Finally, I asked the players if they could find someone to help me, a full-time team manager. Until that happened, I was trying to be everywhere at once and all things to all people.

One day, I was lining the field for a lacrosse game against Wooster College in a black hound's-tooth-print suit from the Piperack. Then I feebly attempted to tape the players' ankles and tried to repair some equipment.

The players were complaining about how Schnoo treated them poorly at practice and during the game, but acted like a friend at other times.

"He's a complicated person," I said after the game, as I walked to my Datsun station wagon elated over the Ten Bears' win over Wooster, 15 to 2. My suit was muddied and stained with the chalk from lining the field. "I'll speak to him," I screamed back to the players standing outside the locker room doors.

I didn't have time to speak to Schnoo about it, and, besides, I figured the situation would resolve itself. It didn't. The players' animosity toward Schnoo grew, and they soon began plotting ways to teach him a lesson.

O

Morgan was "killing" the Amherst lacrosse team, and their players were distraught. The Bears' defense was huge. Football players Bruce Caraway and Harold Bell were well over 6'4" tall and at least 260 pounds, yet agile and quick. Val Emery, an All-State defenseman in high school, had helped the guys with the fundamentals of lacrosse. But it wasn't the Bears' finesse with the lacrosse stick, it was the physical nature of Morgan's game—especially the presence of Stan Cherry—that had Amherst terrified.

Midfielder Ben Kimbers dodging against Amherst. *(photo: George H. Cook,* Baltimore Sunpapers*)*

Their coach, Peter Good, was very upset, and, at one point, used the word "absurd" after the referee, Matt Swerdloff, penalized one of his players. The referee then tacked on an additional two-minute unsportsmanlike penalty for the coach's remark. I asked the referee why he gave Amherst's coach two minutes just for using the word "absurd."

"The word 'absurd' coming from that Englishman," said Swerdloff, "is like one of your kids calling me a motherfucker."

It was also during this 11 to 4 victory against Amherst that Tony Fulton was dubbed the "Earthman" because he usually ended up on the ground after chasing the ball. His uniform was filthy after every game, but he wore it as a badge of honor since it showed his dogged determination to succeed.

I assigned Andi Arenson and Tony Fulton to escort visiting teams. They'd take the team on a brief campus tour and then to the cafeteria. Black students glared at the all-white teams, and they were intimidated.

Visiting teams stayed in the basement of the Church Refectory and slept on old cots. It was musty, damp, claustrophobic, and had only one shower. It also had rats as big as cats. It was terrifying to visitors who were naive (or cheap) enough to stay on campus. The reverend's office demanded a $20 security deposit from the escorts for the cellar key. Andi always borrowed the money from me, and claimed the deposit was never returned to him.

○

A strange tradition started taking place after games and occasionally at practices. The bigger players would drag certain teammates into the showers and playfully threaten to rape them. Initially, Schnoo and I would intervene, even though we knew the players were just teasing. Cherry usually led the group, whose primary targets were studious, smart, well-spoken, elitist fraternity snobs, and sometimes the white boys. And the prey eventually knew it was a "kibitz," even Oliver Chambers, whom Cherry intensely disliked. He had once overheard Chambers mimicking him and swore revenge. Poor Chambers would live to regret making fun of Cherry.

○

Oliver Chambers was born to a Trinidadian father and British mother who moved to the city of Cambridge on Maryland's scenic Eastern Shore from Trinidad when he was 11 years old. Like his father, Oliver wore his hair in dreadlocks, long before that style became fashionable.

Mrs. Chambers home-tutored Oliver until high school. He was extremely bright, spoke English with a slight Caribbean clip, but had certain behavioral difficulties. He fluctuated from street-smart to country bumpkin, was extremely compulsive, and had a streak of kleptomania. In addition, Chambers was a gifted athlete. While he only participated in athletics during the spring season, he played three sports at once: tennis, track, and lacrosse. And he excelled in each, making All-County in his sophomore, junior, and senior years. Oliver was one of the fastest athletes in Maryland.

Oliver came to Morgan State on a track scholarship. He was a handsome, cocoa-brown, lanky young man who had never been farther than a couple of miles from his parents' home before. Easily led and impressed by the "wild crowd," Chambers lost his scholarship and was placed on disciplinary probation by the middle of his freshman year. It took two visits from his parents, one of which included a severe beating from his dad, before he temporarily got it together.

○

In contrast to Chambers, Miles Harrison Jr. was a dedicated and disciplined student who excelled in all his classes and never let down the team. So I was surprised that spring when he went AWOL from practice. No one had seen Miles for two days before he showed up at practice being led by his roommate, Bob Quarles. Miles had his hand on Quarles' shoulder, wore patches over both eyes, and carried a white cane.

"Miles," I asked, strolling over to him, "where ya been? Why have you missed practice, and what's the story with the getup?"

"Chip, I had this terrible accident; burned my corneas. I'm going to be all right, but . . ."

"Come on, cut the bullshit, Miles," I retorted. "You're the last guy I'd expect to miss two practices. You know how the other guys get away with this. I consider you more dedicated. Then to come on with this ruse, I mean, it's ridiculous!"

But Harrison wasn't pulling my leg.

The Monday of that week while working on a senior honors research project for an advanced biology class, Harrison had sustained flash burns to his corneas. He had been working under ultraviolet lights and had not used protective goggles. Over the next eight to ten hours, his vision became progressively worse until by around midnight, he was totally blind. He and his roommate, Robert Quarles, panicked. Quarles was the Ten Bears' first part-time lacrosse team manager, scorekeeper, and clock-timer. Although rattled, Quarles was able to guide Miles to the campus health center.

Due to the severity of Miles's injuries, and at the request of Miles's parents, he was rushed to the University of Maryland Ophthalmology Center where Dr. Lois Young saw him.

Dr. Young was the first African-American female ophthalmologist in the United States.

After diagnosing ultraviolet flash burns of the corneas, which usually improve on their own within 48 hours, she told Miles, "As soon as you can begin to focus, you can play lacrosse again. But, initially, you'll have to have four eyes," meaning eyeglasses.

Miles missed a third day of practice and then returned for the Swarthmore game wearing very thick glasses. He scored three goals and had two assists. Following the game, which the Bears won 14 to 4, I insisted that Miles wear the glasses all the time. Three days later, Harrison's 20/20 vision returned.

"Chip, I can see fine now. Don't need the glasses."

But I was reluctant to let Miles play without the glasses, especially after his spectacular performance against Swarthmore.

Attackman Miles Harrison Jr. (#11) shoots on goal against Swarthmore while midfielder Maurice Tyler (#15) looks on. *(photo: Sid Brooks)*

"Miles," I ordered, "maybe the glasses help in ways we can't understand. Keep them on."

Miles agreed and tried to practice with the thick lenses. He missed passes, fell down, and twice ran into the back of the goal. Finally, I agreed that his vision without the new glasses would have to do.

○

We were on a roll. Several new recruits and a couple more football players gave the Bears twice the skill and depth from their club year team. Robert Hill, a Long Island native and the center on the football team, was playing great on crease defense, and Danny Bell added speed and experience to the midfield.

The Bears were undefeated after five games, and the fans began coming out. We were getting expanded newspaper and TV coverage, and it was then that the first Ivy League opponent to play at Morgan arrived—Dartmouth.

Defenseman Val Emery clearing the ball against Dartmouth. *(photo: Sid Brooks)*

As the season progressed, I noticed that before every game the referees would ask who Cherry was. Cherry's imposing physical stature was fearsome and his reputation was spreading like wildfire.

During the Dartmouth encounter, Scott Fredericks, one of the refs, threw Cherry out for "roughness." I was bewildered because there was no such lacrosse penalty as just roughness.

"Scotty, was it *unnecessary* roughness?" I asked. We had known each other for years.

The referee snapped back, "No. He didn't do anything illegal. He's just too tough. There are already three Dartmouth players out with broken bones. I've got to put Cherry out of the game for the safety of their team."

"But you can't do that," I yelled, stamping around the field. "He's done nothing illegal!"

"Correct," said Referee Fredericks. "I'm sorry."

"Then I'm playing the game under protest," I shouted as the referee walked away.

I did recognize how rough and intimidating Cherry was on the lacrosse field, and used him as an offensive strategy, especially on face-offs.

The Morgan players who were facing-off would clamp down on opponents' sticks as hard as they could and hold a guy in place until Cherry would come rushing in and crush the other player. This so terrified the opposition that they gave up on many face-offs during the first couple of years that Cherry played lacrosse for the Ten Bears.

During the Dartmouth game, Bernie Ullman, the chief lacrosse referee who was also the chief NFL (National Football League) referee, came out of the stands. His job was to observe games throughout the region, grade the referees, and make sure the schools were in compliance with lacrosse protocol. He asked me why there were several students standing closely around behind the team bench and on the field.

Aghast, I told him, "Listen, Bernie. I line the field and tape ankles. I'm trying to keep score and time for the game; and I'm trying to coach my team. Plus, I just finished arguing with your referees who are making no sense, and you want me to maintain crowd control, too? Why don't *you* tell them to get back?"

Ullman looked over at some of the really tough-looking, big black guys standing around. In the middle of the group was Tiger Davis, who never missed a game. They glared back at Ullman.

"Never mind," he said, and returned to the stands.

With Cherry out of the game, Dartmouth won 10 to 8 . . . and my protest was ignored.

After the Dartmouth game, I walked back across campus with Miles to discuss the option of him staying at Morgan an extra year instead of going to medical school. Miles had one year left of athletic eligibility. I thought he should consider taking advantage of it, even if it meant delaying his med school entrance.

We paused at the Student Union and waved to Tiger Davis, who had left the lacrosse game earlier in order to speak at another protest on campus.

A rally was in motion protesting legislation introduced in the Maryland State capital to combine Morgan with the other state colleges in the metropolitan area (Towson State, UMBC, Coppin State, and the University of Baltimore) to form a proposed Baltimore City State University.

"I'm speaking next," said Tiger, "so I've only got a minute. Sorry you guys lost today, but I'm proud of ya."

Tiger smiled and ran off, leaping up on a temporary platform and stirring the crowd. He was still adding to his "Pardon Me" verses. He began:

pardon the ghetto children
products of your vicious cycle
pardon all black parents
who gave all they had to give
pardon me, again, Mr. A merry ka
my crime is i understand

Tiger had returned to Baltimore to work for Associated Catholic Charities in Edmondson Village. His job was to help work with the community to fight unfair real estate deals. They had aligned against a major landlord family named Goldseker, whom they believed were involved in a neighborhood-destroying practice known as the "Black Tax." Certain realtors were trying to scare white people into moving. They would buy their homes cheaply and sell them to other realtors for three to four times the money. Then, the buying realtors would split the homes up and rent them out as apartments. These realtors were viewed as villains. The Goldsekers really weren't part of this get-rich-at-others'-expense scheme. They had been targeted, but it was just a perception due to certain militant rhetoric. Actually, the Goldsekers took care of the blacks in the community. They helped them with housing, clothes, and food when they didn't have anything. So Tiger decided to work, clandestinely, with the Goldsekers to help organize the community and save the Edmondson Village Shopping Center and the surrounding area for a period of time.

(Morris Goldseker, a Jewish immigrant and Baltimore philanthropist, wanted to establish a powerful and enduring bond be-

tween the African-American and Jewish communities. He set up
the Goldseker Foundation to support programs that would directly
benefit the people of Baltimore. Among the programs is the
Goldseker Fellowship Program, which, since 1976, has given 2.2
million dollars to over 1,000 Goldseker Fellows to continue their
graduate education at Morgan State University.)

○

Sid Brooks, the photographer for Morgan's newspaper,
Spokesman's Sports, was assembling the team for a group picture.
He'd been trying to set the shoot up for a week, but could never get
every player to practice on time. A dedicated ROTC student, Sid
was a stickler for timeliness and efficiency, something the Bear
team was lacking. Actually, the team *never* had everyone at practice all the time on any day.

Just behind the school photographer was DeWayne Wickham,
the Vietnam vet who would appear from time to time snapping
photos of practices and games, and sharing his war pictures with
fellow vets, Poopie and Holley.

"Man," said Tony Fulton, "we've become media darlings
around here. Two photographers at practice!"

"Wake up, Tony," said Dickie Hall, "we don't even get two
fans to come out to some of the games."

○

After practice, Poopie approached me.

"Bubbie's thinking of quitting, Chip," he said.

"Why?" I asked, incredulously. Bubbie, a diminutive freshman attackman, was among a host of pleasant surprises that came
out for the "Bear Ten" in the spring of '71.

"He can't take the practices," said Poopie. "Actually, it's pretty
tough out there for a little fella like Bubbie."

William "Bubbie" Bennett had come to Morgan State via
Edmondson. He and fellow new recruits, Morgan Holley and
Maurice Ashe, raised the number of Edmondson alumni to twelve.

The team could not afford to lose Bubbie, who had taken the
pressure off of Miles Harrison Jr. and Dickie Hall with his stellar
attack play.

Bubbie lived around Memorial Stadium near Levitt's Grocery Store. The Levitts were the parents of lacrosse referee Larry

Levitt, who was an All-State player at City College. He played on that mostly Jewish championship team in '58 and '59, and later was an All-American at University of Maryland. Bubbie grew up with Danny Bell, who lived across the street from the Levitt Grocery and also worked there part-time.

Growing up, Bubbie and Danny Bell were interested in baseball and also played Optimist (Little League) football. Bubbie was very small, but athletic, while Danny had excellent size and excelled in all sports. One day they were watching an older neighbor, Maurice Dorsey, play catch with a lacrosse ball and stick against a wall. (Maurice attended Edmondson and was All-State in lacrosse playing with Wayne, Cherry, and Dickie Hall.) Danny Bell and Bubbie were fascinated and decided to take up lacrosse after that.

Bubbie attended City College High School for two years, but was hanging out with a bad crowd. He cut a lot of classes, got into some minor trouble, and, due to poor grades, had to go to summer school. His mother was very upset, so to keep him out of trouble, she had Bubbie transferred to Edmondson where he finished his high school career as an honor student.

Bubbie played J.V. lacrosse at City, but in his last two years at Edmondson High, he played varsity with a strong, silent defenseman named Maurice Ashe.

Danny Bell was a three-sport star at City College High School. He was a tight end and made high school All-American in football. He also played varsity basketball and lacrosse. He was a very tough player and a good student. Danny received numerous football scholarship offers.

However, a teacher at City named Ray Banks, who was the son of Coach Earl Banks, influenced Bell. "Papa Bear" came by City one day and recruited Danny.

Bubbie and Danny Bell arrived at Morgan State in the fall of 1970. Bubbie went out for lacrosse that spring. At only 5'4" tall and 125 pounds, Bubbie was extremely intimidated by the immenseness of the Morgan lacrosse team, which included over a dozen football players. Bubbie was especially terrified of Cherry, who loved to run around hitting people with his body and his stick. Cherry was a great instigator, but Bubbie took it. He played well and was respected. And he could handle the stick right- and left-handed.

Bubbie despised practice. He would rather play other teams for hours than practice at Morgan because of the brutal physicality of the scrimmages.

I finally convinced Bubbie to signal me when he could no longer tolerate Cherry, and I would immediately substitute for Bubbie without anyone knowing why.

Meanwhile, Danny Bell and Cherry became close friends. They hung out together and double-dated a lot. While they argued often and wrestled around, they remained good buddies. Stanley was just a kid and acted like a child. He'd slap someone on the head and argue with him, but was primarily joking around. However, his scowl and size conjured up great fear in people's imaginations and caused them to approach Stanley with trepidation.

Influenced by Cherry, Danny, who arrived at Morgan a mature man, regressed into immaturity.

○

Miles Harrison Jr. was home discussing the success of Morgan's first varsity season with his dad, a Chemistry and Biology teacher. I was anxious to know if he was returning next year or graduating. If he left Morgan, he'd still be the first player from a black college ever selected to the prestigious North/South All-Star Game. But if he returned in 1972, there was the prospect of playing on an even better team.

"I've got one more year of eligibility left and I'm leaning towards staying at Morgan another year. We've got the nucleus to make the NCAA Tournament," explained Miles.

His dad was quiet for over two minutes before speaking. "Son, you've already been accepted to the University of Pennsylvania Medical School. If you go this year, you'll get out early and begin a career quicker. Everyone in the family is so proud of you. They wouldn't understand this lacrosse thing. Plus you could get hurt . . ."

"But, Dad . . ." interrupted Miles.

"Let me finish," said Harrison Sr. sternly. "I've watched you play. Big guys pounding on your arms and hands—and I know you've got protective equipment on, but it's not enough. You play with reckless abandon. Hell, someone could break your fingers, fracture your skull. It's not worth it, son. Think with your head, not your balls!"

And, as much as Miles wanted to play one more year, he knew his dad was right. He agreed to graduate.

O

It was another very rough practice, and John Madden, the coach of the NFL Oakland Raiders, who was planning on drafting Ray Chester (football and novice lacrosse player), was watching. He stood on the sidelines and mimicked the noise. "Boom, crack, bang! What a rough game this is! Hey, don't use my guy Chester. We're thinking of drafting him. What kind of game is this?" Madden's stream-of-consciousness chattering became his trademark years later when he became a popular television network sportscaster.

O

For those who knew me, it was funny to watch me coach since I came from the "do as I say, not as I do" school. From a player's perspective, I was a very persistent coach in terms of forcing the team to be in great shape. A stickler for fundamentals, I went over the most minute facets of the game time and time again. As a result, my players were in as good or better shape than any team they ever played against, excelling in speed, endurance, and the fundamentals of the game of lacrosse. Additionally, I constantly stressed the importance of practicing on one's own.

My relationship with the team was unique. I spoke to and dealt with the players in a way that was totally different from any of their previous coaches. Instead of being pedantic and aloof, I was approachable and understanding. I was probably more of a psychologist in my coaching technique than anything else. I believed that I related much better than other coaches to the players, and was as concerned about their mental and emotional states as their physical condition. The players realized that I cared—although they knew that I wasn't one to mess with too often. I was also hip enough to know if the players were bullshitting me (half of the time).

O

Oliver Chambers was forgetful. During practices or games, he always lost a shoe, stick, armpad, or something needed to play. It held up practice, and greatly aggravated me, but amused the players.

Cherry loved to scare Oliver. He was always threatening to beat him up or rape him. During the Loyola game, while the team was in the huddle during a time-out, Stanley kept smiling over at Oliver and looking at his rear end. "I'm gonna get you, Ollie," he warned.

After the game, which the Bears won 9 to 1, Chambers begged Wayne to escort him into the shower and stand guard while he washed up.

"Oliver," said Wayne, "he's only joking around."

"It don't matter," said Chambers. "He's so crazy, he might just carry out his threat to impress the rest of you guys."

All the guys knew it was good to have Cherry on your side.

The Morgan auditorium was packed for a meeting protesting two issues: the killing of two students at a historically black college in Mississippi during an antiwar march, and a Free Ochiki Young rally. Students and concerned citizens from the metropolitan area were in attendance.

Cherry was seated next to Andi and his friend, a beautiful black coed from Chicago. Stanley was more concerned about the coed than any antiwar protest.

Desmond X, the first speaker, opened the meeting. "I want all undesirables to leave, now!" His meaning was crystal clear. The white people in attendance got up and left to thunderous applause from the audience.

Andi began to rise, but Cherry ordered him to sit back down. Playing to the crowd, an aggressive student in the row behind demanded that Andi leave. Cherry stood, leaned over his seat, and spoke to the instigator. "Three things I gotta say. One, he's a Morgan student, and two, he's with me."

Cherry moved to sit back down when the instigator tapped him and said, "You forgot 'three.' What's three?"

"Just this," answered Cherry as he turned around and punched the instigator over his seat into the next row.

During one practice, Stanley Cherry wanted to take the ball away from Wayne Jackson to show off for the guys. It was towards the end of practice, and many of the players were egging Stanley on. However, Wayne made him look bad, chiding him. "You can't get this; I'm the best." He was protecting the ball where there was no way that Stanley could legitimately get to it.

Stanley began swinging his stick wildly out of frustration until he hit Wayne in the side of the shin and busted a blood vessel. It was the closest they ever came to a fight in all the years they had grown up together. They were in each other's faces. Fortunately, no one took the first swing, and they eventually left together and slept at Stanley's that night.

O

Pregame rituals developed as the season progressed. Andi took vitamin C before each game, telling Wayne it was LSD. Some guys greased up with "Red Hot," a salve, to keep their legs warm. Guys would sometimes put Red Hot in Tony Bullock's jockstrap, but only during practice. Holley would read supposedly inspirational messages from an esoteric book and then try to explain them; but no one generally followed. And then there was the ritual of watching Cherry tape his massive cock to his leg. He felt this provided better protection than the standard issue jockstrap that he claimed wasn't large enough to hold his "gems."

O

Though the season had gotten off to a great start and the team was constantly improving, our luck was about to change.

A key game was approaching against UMBC, and I was going over the scouting report. I ascertained that the key to their offense was Doug Fry, a left-handed, tough crease attackman who was leading the nation in scoring.

Robert Hill, the center on the football team, was the Bears' crease defenseman, and I needed him to guard a "lefty" all week to prepare for the game.

"Tatum," I ordered, "you'll be Fry all this week."

Clyde Tatum was a left-handed attackman who had played with Miles Harrison Jr. at Forest Park. He was somewhat jaded, drank too much, and hung with a bad crowd, but he was really a good guy, albeit a bit unlucky. Clyde idolized Miles from high school, and when he came to Morgan, he couldn't wait to pledge Harrison's fraternity, Kappa Alpha Psi (a.k.a. the Kappas).

Val Emery and Miles came from the black bourgeoisie and were part of the Kappas, an elite Greek fraternity. Their families wielded tremendous influence at the school, and that was how they were able to "convince" Coach Banks to consider a lacrosse team.

Clyde was a great cheerleader for the team and gave a hundred percent all the time. So his reaction to my request was strange.

"I ain't playing no white guy!"

"Clyde, it's just a mock practice. We really need to go over it," I pleaded.

"No," insisted Clyde.

"All right. Pritchett, you do it," I ordered. George Pritchett was a swift midfielder from Annapolis.

"Hell no!" screamed Pritchett. "I ain't no Uncle Tom!"

"Okay, forget it," I said, totally frustrated. "Schnoo, you'll play Fry all week."

"Why me?" asked Schnoo. "I'm much taller than him."

"Because you're white," I answered.

"But," said Schnoo, "Fry is a natural left-hander and I'm not. Chip, you'll have to play him since you're the only natural lefty here."

The players stared at me, awaiting my response.

"But I'm wearing a suit and dress shoes . . ." And with that I ran onto the field to play crease attack.

Big mistake. Every time the ball was thrown to me or I tried to dodge in, the players would converge, especially Cherry. I was repeatedly checked, slashed, and knocked down until I called an early end to practice.

UMBC beat the Bears 18 to 8, and Fry had a field day.

○

Undefeated Division I powerhouse Hofstra was visiting Morgan in a key match-up and had thrown its famous zone defense against us. It was causing scoring difficulties. Coach Banks and some of his assistant football coaches stood near the team bench and wondered aloud why I wasn't allowing Wayne to dodge through everyone like he usually did. I tried to explain the lacrosse zone defense to them and my strategy against it (passing the ball around and not trying to dodge in), and coach the team at the same time. Not an easy task. Hofstra won in a closer game than expected.

○

Morgan finished its maiden varsity season winning ten out of fourteen games. Everyone was very impressed with the way the team played, and looked forward to 1972.

Wayne Jackson made All-American, and Miles Harrison Jr. was chosen to play in the North/South All-Star Game.

The North/South All-Star Game was alternately played in a Northern or Southern site, and this year's location was Tufts University in Massachusetts. Miles was selected for the South team. Most of Miles's experience with racism was from a Southern perspective, and he considered the North to be more liberal. However, he discovered that Northerners could be just as racist.

There was an even number of players on the team, so everyone should have been paired with a roommate. Miles, however, found himself in a single room. The only other single room was for a white player from Ohio Wesleyan University named Jim Lips. When they realized what was going on, the two decided to room together.

The next evening, there was a welcoming clambake for the players at Alumni Hall. Miles was introduced to many locals, officials, and participants. There were cordial handshakes but no conversation. Lips was shocked at this behavior. He hung around a lot with Miles and tried to smooth things out.

MILES HARRISON
Morgan State   5-10/162   Midfield
Scored 23 goals and 16 assists this year . . . Dean's List student for four years in Pre-Med course.

Photo and stats of Miles Harrison Jr. from the 1971 North/ South Lacrosse All-Star Game's *Official Program Book.*

At the game, attackman/midfielder Miles excelled. He was the fastest player and, eventually, was grudgingly given the respect he deserved.

○

Athletic Director Banks was reviewing the lacrosse season in his office with me. I was asking for athletic scholarships for next season.

"Because of our success," I said, "white schools are now going after good black lacrosse players. We have to be more competitive. Also, I received this letter and photo of a great prospect from Hempstead High in Long Island. A Salvation Army Youth League director, a Morgan alum, recommended this kid, Dave Raymond."

"Lemme see those, Sibman," said Banks. "He looks kinda small."

I leaned forward in my chair. "He's also an outstanding football defensive back," I said. "I've checked Raymond out with a buddy of mine who coaches on the Island. There are a couple other players I'm scouting, too. I'll need about five scholarships."

"I'll give ya one 'ship, Chip. You can split it three ways."

Sliding dejectedly back into my chair, I pleaded, "Coach Banks, I'll never get Raymond with a partial scholarship. He's already got a full ride to Shippensburg State."

Coach Banks smiled and held up one finger. "One 'ship. That's it! Split it or give it all to the kid from Long Island . . . By the way, wanna buy some raffle tickets? We're having the drawing at my bar in Northwood tonight. It's for a good cause. They're $25 apiece. How many ya want?"

"I'll take one," I said reluctantly.

"You'll take four," ordered Banks. "I just gave you a scholarship . . . Say, Sibman, that's a nice suit you got, but you need to get it cleaned. Ya got all that chalk, lime, and mud on it. It's not a good image."

○

Earl Banks took over the head football coaching job at Morgan during a period when the team was considered practically unbeatable, and he kept them that way for a long time.

When I arrived at Morgan to work in the graduate school, Coach Banks' football team began an undefeated streak that lasted almost four years. He was also responsible for a huge financial boon for Morgan athletics in an annual Urban League game that was played in Yankee Stadium against Grambling University.

Anytime I was in the presence of Coach Banks, I felt I was on holy ground. Banks was on a par with Vince Lombardi, George Hallas, Bear Bryant, and Eddie Robinson.

But, by the early 1970s, the football program began to wane. The undefeated seasons ceased. Morgan started losing games, and the losses seemed to grow every year. It didn't seem that a turnaround could be expected. The coach had also taken on the responsibility as athletic director for Morgan State.

I approached Earl Banks in his bar one night toward the end of the spring and asked, "Coach, what's happening with the football team? I notice you've been losing lately, and it doesn't seem like the old Morgan teams. I'm also hearing this talk about you retiring from football."

Banks stood there shaking his head, then came around from behind the bar. He was a short, squat man, perhaps 5'9" and weighing 240 pounds. Slowly, he walked over and sat on a stool next to me.

"Sibman, the players have changed. It used to be we had the pick of any black kid in America. If they didn't come to Morgan, they went to one of the rival historically black schools: Grambling, Tennessee State, Florida A & M . . . But today it's different. The white colleges and universities are offering all kinds of money and incentives. And who knows what else." He was alluding to the fact that big-time football in America had other perks, such as money, cars, and women.

"So I don't get my 'pick of the litter' like I used to. Not only that, the kids who come here have developed a different attitude. Used to be when I'd tell a kid to run into a brick wall, he would ask, 'How fast do you want me to run into that brick wall, Coach?' Well, today it's different. When I ask a kid to run into a brick wall, he says to me, 'Well, Coach, let me see. That brick wall is made of mortar, rock, and cement that has been seriously hardened; and if I run into that wall at 10, 15, or 20 miles an hour, there are certain muscles and bones that will break.' So you see, Sibman, they don't listen anymore. They're thinking too much, and they *think* they know too much."

SUMMER 1971

Dave Raymond visited Morgan State with his parents and girlfriend. She was definitely going to Shippensburg State, but he was waffling since he had received a letter from Athletic Director Banks and me offering him a full lacrosse scholarship.

In my absence, Wayne Jackson was there to take Dave around. They talked about the black college experience and Morgan's sports program. Wayne also let Dave know that the ratio of females to males at Morgan was six to one.

Much to the chagrin of his girlfriend, Dave announced on the car ride back to New York that he would be attending Morgan State.

○

That summer, as part of my job for the State Drug Abuse Administration, I was in Maryland's number-one beach resort, Ocean City, meeting with my boss, the Secretary of the State Department of Health. We were discussing a deadly drug epidemic. Some drug dealers were selling a drug called the Sunshine Pill (supposedly a speedy version of LSD), which contained strychnine, to unsuspecting teenagers.

The Drug Abuse Administration contracted an airplane to fly over the beach towing a sign that read: "The Sunshine Pill Kills." We also alerted the media. The day of the plane's virgin voyage, key state officials were stationed on the beach ready to give sound bites about the anti-Sunshine Pill program and their general cleverness and concern. The plane flew over the ocean along the coastline. Everyone began to point to it. Somehow, the sign became entangled in the plane's wing. The propellers sputtered, the engine stopped, and the plane crashed into the ocean, quickly ending its "big" media kickoff. Cheers went up from the beach.

○

While Wayne was at Morgan State, his old high school coach asked him to help Marvin Webster, a very tall basketball player, improve his footwork. He wanted Marvin to try and guard Wayne, who was almost a foot shorter but much quicker. Wayne had a very quick first step and could roll by Marvin every time. Plus, Webster couldn't block any of Wayne's shots.

At seven feet tall, Marvin had not yet "grown into" his height. Gangly and awkward, he had tremendous potential. Wayne and Marvin were dedicated neighborhood guys who were very loyal to Edmondson High School. Webster also hung around with Bubbie, who he referred to as "Shorty."

That summer, Wayne recruited Marvin to attend Morgan. He convinced Marvin that it was better to attend Morgan State where he could develop at a slower pace and eventually play more than to go to the University of Maryland or any other high-profile college. Wayne also gave Marvin advice on how to negotiate his basketball scholarship with the Athletic Department.

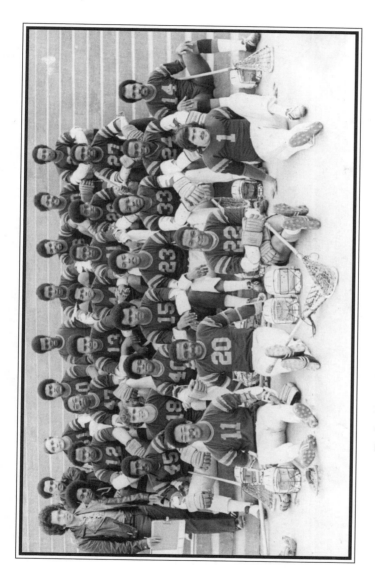

The first Morgan State College varsity lacrosse team — the 1971 Bears.

CHAPTER 6

CHALLENGING THE "IVORY" LEAGUE

FALL 1971

As good an athlete as he was in high school, wild, egotistical Danny Bell was, however, a step behind the truly great players at Morgan. But Danny believed he was better than anyone.

Morgan was playing a football game at South Caroline State, and the day before the game, Danny Bell went to get Wayne and Stanley, who were hanging out in the visiting team dormitory. He told them, "Come on out to the patio. There are two fine-looking ladies out there. They're going to get their other girlfriend, and it looks like they could be easy conquests."

Stanley and Wayne went out back and found Danny squeezing and dancing with a beautiful girl in short-shorts and thigh-high boots. She had the most beautiful legs they had ever seen. Wayne and Stanley sat on a ledge and chatted with the other girl. Suddenly the new girlfriend came down the steps. She went over and introduced herself to Wayne and Stanley.

Wayne and Stanley looked at each other and began shaking her hands. They weren't exactly sure, but her big hands kind of gave away that she wasn't "all" girl. They looked around to confirm their hunches and realized that all the girls were really men. They began laughing at Danny Bell, who was necking like crazy while dancing closer and closer with the long-legged "girl" in the short-shorts.

They called Danny over and whispered, "They're faggots, you fool!" Danny didn't believe them. He went over to his date, reached down, and grabbed her crotch. He felt a cock and went berserk, sucker-punching "her" in the face. Meanwhile, Stanley and Wayne raced back to the dormitory to tell all the players about Danny's "walk on the wild side." He was teased unmercifully the rest of the season.

○

I was trying to get funding for new lacrosse equipment from the athletic director. "Sorry, champ (one of his generic pet names)," said Banks, "there's no money."

But instead of accepting the "no" response, I casually re-marked that I'd go over and ask the president's office. I'd found that Banks would rather approve my request than get a call from the academic side of the campus.

○

My first-ever lacrosse scholarship recruit, Dave Raymond, enrolled at Morgan and looked forward to playing football, too. Dave was an excellent defensive back, but the coaches wouldn't let him try out for the football team because he was too small.

Dave Raymond was heavily recruited by Shippensburg State University, which had football and basketball programs, but no lacrosse. Dave's high school basketball coach was a graduate of Shippensburg, which was trying hard to recruit minorities. They tried to use Dave's high school, Hempstead High, as a pipeline for that purpose. But Dave had opted for Morgan State.

Good-looking and extremely cool, Dave had a steady stream of coed visitors after he moved into his dormitory.

Born in Queens, New York, Dave had three brothers and one sister. His father managed hotel chains for over 40 years, and his mother was an elementary school teacher. In 1959, the Raymonds moved to Hempstead, Long Island where Mrs. Raymond taught.

Dave attended Hempstead High from 1967 to 1971. As a freshman, he played football, basketball, and lacrosse. He be-came interested in lacrosse by playing in a summer league before attending high school. Dave hung around with some older guys who taunted him about having to leave baseball, an early love of his, for lacrosse. By his junior year, Dave was playing varsity football, basketball, and lacrosse. He started on attack in lacrosse

Morgan's first out-of-state lacrosse recruit, attackman Dave Raymond from Long Island. *(photo: Sid Brooks)*

and became an All-Nassau County player during his junior and senior years. Hempstead High won three division championships and lost in the finals of the county championships to Massapequa High.

During the summers, Dave played in a lacrosse summer league for high school and college players in Freeport, Long Island, a couple miles from the beach. Dave's team primarily recruited black players, though they had some white and Hispanic players as well. They consistently won their division, but ultimately lost in the second or third round of the playoffs. The games were very competitive and there were always fights. After the games, everyone would put aside on-field differences and drive down to the beach for keg parties where they had a great time. There were some topnotch players from Long Island who played in this league, and competing against them helped develop Dave's game. A minimum of 20 teams participated. Dave's high school buddies, the three "M" Guys: Mendoza, Mug, and Maceo, also played summer league lacrosse, and later joined him at Morgan in '74 and '75.

○

The fall of 1971 was unusually cooler than what normally engulfed Baltimore.

Tiger Davis caught up with me leaving the Athletic Department office in Hurt Gymnasium and informed me that H. Rap Brown had been arrested in New York. He'd been a fugitive for 17 months.

"According to the cops, Rap and three buddies tried to rob the Red Carpet Lounge in Manhattan," said Tiger.

"Guess he was desperate," I said.

"Maybe," said Tiger. "According to my sources, they were really looking to rip off this drug dealer who hung at the bar. When they couldn't ID him, they decided to rob the patrons."

"How'd they catch him?" I asked.

"Looks like someone informed because a bunch of cops were waiting as they left the bar," said Tiger. "A gun battle ensued and Rap was shot."

"Is he okay?" I asked.

"Yeah," said Tiger. "He's in Roosevelt Hospital recovering from gunshot wounds."

○

Cherry and Wayne were standing at a bus stop near Edmondson Village hitchhiking to Morgan. Neither could afford a car, and bus fare could substitute for lunch. As the early morning drivers pulled up to the stoplight where they stood, they pushed down the locks of their car doors and stared straight ahead.

Later, in the locker room after football practice, Cherry stood up, grabbed his back, and passed out. There was no medical help for him, or any of the other athletes at Morgan State. (This was traditional of many financially underfunded colleges.) All right, there was an elderly Jamaican physician who stopped by on occasion, but . . .

I found out about Cherry's injury from Wayne, and took him over to see my friend Dr. Larry Becker (an orthopedic surgeon and former lacrosse star at Hopkins), who recommended an immediate operation. Cherry had a ruptured disc that had split from the plate in his back. Becker sent him to see a neurosurgeon, Dr. Neil Aaronson, who examined him and scheduled an operation. Cherry was in excruciating pain.

Most people would be crippled for life from this injury and certainly would not be able to move around, so Aaronson and Becker couldn't believe it when Cherry casually strolled into the Sinai Hospital lobby the day of his operation.

○

Dave Raymond's girlfriend from Shippensburg came to visit for Homecoming. After the game, she and Dave went back to his dorm room, which he shared with three other students. Theirs was a popular room, with many female visitors traipsing in and out. This exposure to Dave's life at Morgan was too much for his girlfriend. She quickly decided to end their relationship and returned to Shippensburg State.

○

Camilla Yates, better known as Millie, grew up in northwest Baltimore. She was an athletic child, considered the fastest girl in her neighborhood. She had on occasion even run down thieves who had stolen other kids' bikes. Periodically, Millie would travel with family friends to Clifton Park in east Baltimore to race against other girls from all over the city in the Bureau of Recreation track meets.

Millie attended Northwestern High School where she ran track, competing in the 100-yard dash and the 440-yard dash. She was also a member of the school's excellent 440-yard dash relay team. In addition, she was an outstanding cheerleader.

A good student, Millie planned to attend Frostburg State University in Western Maryland, but her application arrived too late and she had to settle for Morgan State. Northwestern High had a theater arts major, and Millie was part of that program. She wanted to further her education at Frostburg State, which also had an excellent theater arts program and a culturally diverse student body. Millie loved the fact that at Northwestern, and hopefully at Frostburg, she could continue her relationships with white students and other ethnic groups.

In high school, Millie hung out with the jocks. She attended every game or meet, regardless of the sport: football, basketball, swimming, track, and lacrosse. She came home late every night because she had been at all of the competitions.

In the fall of 1971, Millie began classes at Morgan State. She commuted from home the first semester. Naive and generally conservative, Millie would leave a party immediately if there was marijuana around. Although initially shy, she was a very friendly person and got along with everyone. Millie had a nice figure, though slightly overweight, with chocolate-brown skin and an effervescent smile.

Millie had a lot of friends in the freshmen dormitory at Baldwin Hall where she first saw Dave Raymond. She was there visiting classmates, studying, or trying to keep her girlfriend, Linda, a cheerleader, out of trouble. Actually, once she met Dave, Millie and Linda had him believing that they were sisters.

Every time Millie saw Dave, he was wearing the same jacket that his friend Mendoza Wallace had sent him from Farmingdale Community College. It was a beautiful athletic jacket and had the name "Andy" emblazoned over the heart. Millie thought for the longest time that Raymond's first name was Andy.

WINTER 1971

At my second USILA Convention, I scheduled Syracuse and a host of other Division I teams. Suddenly, I was more popular. An NCAA lacrosse tournament had been set up, and if a team had a good record and played a strong schedule, they would be selected. A game against Morgan fit the bill for both. Again, though, William and Mary refused to play Morgan because it was a historically black institution.

At a team meeting, I told the players that the prognostications looked great for the coming year. I also informed the team about the new NCAA tournament format.

○

Wayne Jackson loved basketball and wanted to play at Morgan. He was working out with some varsity players one day, unaware that the soon-to-retire basketball coach, Brutus Wilson, was watching. Wayne was sinking all of his shots and was very impressive. Coach Wilson approached him and asked, "Do you play like that all the time? If you do, how 'bout coming out for the team?" Wayne agreed and Coach Wilson informed him that he would talk to Coach Banks. Wayne was elated.

But Banks deflated Coach Wilson. "No, I need a fullback, and I don't want Wayne playing any other sports."

"But he's already playing lacrosse," pleaded Wilson.

"I can't keep Wayne from lacrosse," lamented Banks. "He's their best player—one of the best around. The other side of Cold Spring Lane wouldn't allow it." He was referring to the administration and academic faculty.

○

Some of the players and I were visiting Cherry in the hospital when Dr. Becker came by. He explained to me that Cherry was basically a Superman, referring to his impressive recovery. I interjected, "Yeah, that's true, Dr. Becker. I've seen him eat chili dogs at halftime and then play the game right after that." Becker looked at me quizzically.

SPRING 1972

Everything looked great entering the '72 season. Practice began early and the team was out sloshing in the snow. Courtenay Servary, a freshman Other-Race recruit, looked good playing around in the goal. However, he had been penciled in to play midfield.

Dave Raymond was a great natural athlete, but never worked out outside of practice and games. Recognizing speed and endurance as essentials in lacrosse, I was a taskmaster at having the team run both long distances and short sprints, before and after practice. Unlike many players who griped at the conditioning program, Dave enjoyed it as someone in top condition might.

○

In a rare departure for a state prosecutor, Richard J. Kinlein, the Howard County state's attorney, filed a motion for a speedy trial for H. Rap Brown. According to Kinlein, the "inciting" charges against Brown appeared lacking in evidence and fabricated.

News of the prosecutor's remarks was widespread and, after practice, was a major topic of discussion.

"I hope Rap gets off, but I don't get it," said Poopie, walking off the field after practice. "He went to Cambridge, spoke and marched; and then there was shootin', lootin', and burnin'. If that ain't incitin' . . ."

"It ain't," interrupted Oliver Chambers. "I mean, he didn't incite. I was there; I know. I'm from Cambridge."

Several players gathered around Oliver in awe.

"How old were you?" asked Andi.

"Fifteen," responded Oliver, "and I was with Rap all night long."

Danny Bell got up in Chambers' face.

"You're full of shit!" he exclaimed. "No way you were next to Rap all night."

"Hey man, I wasn't attached to him," said Oliver, "but I was in the crowd and saw everything."

Poopie "cooled out" Bell. "Go ahead, Chambers, tell us what happened."

"It was the last week of July in '67, and there were about 400 black folk listening to speeches and waiting for Rap Brown."

"Four hundred?" asked Bell. "How many Negroes live in Cambridge?"

"About 4,000." said Oliver. "Almost a third of the city.

"Anyhow, Rap showed up an hour late. There were cops everywhere. Black cops who patrolled our community, and white cops and National Guardsmen in front of all the stores on Race Street.

"Race Street divided the black and white communities. Rap Brown got up on top of this car and started shouting, 'Take your violence to the honkies . . . get some guns . . . burn Cambridge down! It's time for Cambridge to explode, baby. Black folks built America, and if America don't come around, we're going to burn America down!' People cheered and cheered, and that was it. The crowd kinda broke up and people headed home."

"Then what?" inquired Poopie.

"A lot of us were just hanging around when some girl asked Rap and a couple of guys to walk her home. She lived near Race Street and was afraid of the white cops. Me and some buddies watched as they walked this girl up the street. Suddenly, shooting started. It came from the bushes and everyone ducked."

Bell, who'd been sitting on the grass, jumped up. "Who was it? Klansmen, the National Guard, white cops?!"

"Actually," responded Oliver almost sheepishly, "it was black policemen."

"No shit," a surprised Bell exclaimed.

"Yeah," said Oliver. "Rap got shot, but it was only a graze in his head by a shotgun pellet.

"After the shooting, people got real mad. Some got their guns, and some began tearing up everything. A white cop got shot in the neck, face, and hand. Later, they burned this elementary school down. And then they stopped white people who had mistakenly drove into the neighborhood. Brothers pulled them out of cars, beat them, and burned their cars . . . But nobody got killed."

"Why'd they burn their own elementary school down?" interrupted Andi.

"It was rat infested and deteriorating," answered Oliver.

"What happened to Rap?" asked Poopie.

"Different people hid him in their homes until someone drove him to Washington.

"So, really," added Oliver, "he didn't incite the riot. If the cops hadn't started shooting, nothing would've happened. At least not that night . . ."

O

A few days into the second semester, Dave Raymond was walking across a bridge on his way to the athletic fields when he saw a young lady, bent over, speaking to someone in a car parked under the end of the bridge. It was Millie. She was wearing hiphugger bell-bottom jeans that accentuated her curves. Dave realized it was Millie when she stood up. For the first time, he realized how beautiful she really was. She had lost that somewhat chubby look from the first semester. Shy Millie chatted with Dave, letting him know that she was moving into an apartment.

"That's great," said Dave. "You've got a new car, too. Right?"

Dave helped Millie move into her new apartment, and that's where he met her parents. They thought Dave was a wonderful young man and didn't even mind when Millie loaned him her car.

Every now and then Millie would stop by Dave's dorm room to visit. If she didn't find him, she would tape a dime to his door meaning, "Just call me." At first their relationship was platonic.

Then, one evening, Millie had Dave over for dinner and, later, asked him to spend the night. That was the beginning of their romance. She was also hotly pursued by many young men around the campus. Her blending-into-the-background days were over.

Millie was not possessive of Dave and let him have his space. She put no limitations on him. There was no jealously, and Dave didn't pressure her, either. They were discovering each other and themselves during this coming-of-age period.

Millie became queen of one of the fraternities, a very prestigious position. She was in the limelight and quite a popular figure on campus. As the fraternity queen of Omega Psi Phi, nicknamed "The Q's," she achieved enormous attention. In addition, she had become a varsity cheerleader.

○

Oliver Chambers negotiated a deal with me to help line the field and perform other team maintenance duties in return for a seat in the front of the bus for away games. He was afraid that Cherry and others would mess with him in the rear of the bus.

Chambers enlisted the aid of a guy named "Butterfly" who was adept with a switchblade knife. He used this talent to slice up butterfly bandages to stop bleeding lacrosse wounds. He became the team trainer and Oliver's assistant.

During this time, Oliver frequently had Vicks inhalers stuck up his nose. Only later did I realize that they might have contained cocaine.

○

Out of the hospital for a few weeks, Cherry was arguing with some football teammates over who would ride shotgun in a car going to an on-campus party. Frustrated, Cherry eventually grabbed the two big guys, both offensive linemen, lifted them over his head, and threw them out onto the street. It was obvious that he was feeling better.

○

I was informed the day before the first game of the '72 season that seven of my starters were ineligible. Athletic Director Banks told me that these seven had signed professional football contracts, making them ineligible to play college lacrosse even though it was a different sport. This was one of the last years that this rule was on the books. After that, the National Collegiate Athletic Association changed the rule to state that if an athlete signed to play a pro sport, he couldn't participate in the *same* sport in college. Other than that, he could play another sport. This drastically altered Morgan's aspirations for 1972, and led to our only losing season. It did, however, allow many other players, who would shape the Ten Bears' destiny for the three years to follow, to gain experience and exposure.

O

As in ice hockey and soccer, the most crucial position in lacrosse is the goalie. The goalie must have super quick reflexes so that he can block a hard rubber ball coming toward him at over 100 miles per hour. He must then take control of the ball and direct clearing it out of his defensive position within a matter of seconds. When the opposition is conducting its plays on offense, the goalie must speak clearly, loudly, and quickly to his defensive teammates, informing them of where the ball is, where the opponents are setting picks, and if a shot has been fired. Without a very good and consistent goalie, a team cannot vie for a championship.

It wasn't until early in the third season that Morgan would discover the goalie of its dreams. During the first year as a club team, the Bears used a converted Edmondson High defenseman named David Lewis, since there were no players with pure goalie experience. David was, at best, inconsistent. On bad days, he was sievelike—everything thrown his way went right through him. But when he was "on," he was awesome. In a game midway through the 1970 season against a University of Maryland "B" team that included many varsity members, Lewis stopped almost every shot. Morgan lost late in the game by a couple of goals, but without David's excellent blocking we would never have gotten that close. Maryland was 10 to 20 goals better, but David Lewis was impenetrable.

In 1971, a white midfielder, Essex Community College transfer Bruce Herling, decided to try out for goalie and proved to be a pleasant surprise. Although only an average talent, Bruce had a big heart, and he brought leadership and consistency to the defense. His only flaw was that he'd lose his cool on occasion—when a bad shot went in or a player missed an assignment—and the floodgates would open.

Morgan's defense surrounding the goalie was neither as skilled nor as consistent as some of its major opponents, so the Bears' goalie was not exactly at fault when he was continually faced with point-blank shots. Those days made Bruce yearn to play midfield again.

Morgan State goalie, #13, Courtenay Servary.

Courtenay Servary, all five-foot-three-inches of him, came to Morgan on an Other-Race Grant expecting a chance to play midfield, though he had excelled as a goalie in high school.

For a white kid, Courtenay's life played like a melodrama of an urban minority waif. Adopted from an orphanage at the age of five, he lived with his parents on a farm in north Baltimore County near the Pennsylvania border. For the first few years, things were fine.

Courtenay attended his father's alma mater, Boys' Latin, a private school in the city, where he was taught to play lacrosse and ice hockey. Back home, he learned mechanical skills from his neighbors, two elderly brothers who owned a 145-acre farm.

But in the late '60s, his parents divorced, and they lost the farm to creditors. Courtenay moved to a small apartment in the city with his mother. Their relationship became strained. Courtenay was attending Northern High School, which, due to overcrowding, had instituted double shifts. He went to classes from eight a.m. to twelve noon, and worked in a department store as a stock boy and driver from one to nine p.m. Following numerous domestic confrontations, he decided to leave his mother's flat.

Courtenay moved in with a schoolmate named Buddy, and they planned to join the Army and fly "choppers" in Vietnam. A week before he was to formally sign his induction papers, Courtenay decided to attend Morgan and play college lacrosse instead. (His friend, Buddy, enlisted anyway and piloted refugees out during the evacuation of Saigon.)

O

At the beginning of the '72 season, I started Bruce in the goal and allowed Courtenay his wish, especially since I had never seen him play goalie and considered him a good but small midfield prospect. That was until a preseason scrimmage one evening in early March against Carling Lacrosse Club, an outstanding club team of former All-Americans that constantly vied for the U.S. Club title. Carling was led by player/coach Arly Marshall, an Army major.

The game was played under the lights by the Calvary parade grounds at Fort Meade, Maryland. It was an eerie setting, playing in cold rain and mist on a manure-laden field with the Army barracks backdrop. Clearly outmanned, Morgan could not stop the onslaught of goals by Carling.

Finally, Courtenay approached me. "Let me get in the goal. I'm not getting any action running midfield, anyhow, since the ball's been in our defensive end all day."

With that, I switched Bruce with Courtenay, who proceeded to stop the next 20 shots taken by Carling. Balls were flying everywhere—high right, low left, skip bounces, corner pipe shots—it didn't matter. Servary was smothering everything. Here was this five-foot-three one-hundred-thirty-pounder covering a six-by-six goal like a tarpon. He was incredible! In addition, Courtenay was able to clear the ball up into our offensive zone, and we even managed to score a few goals before the night mercifully ended.

That was it for me! Watching Courtenay's play in the goal, against some of the greatest offensive attackmen and midfielders in lacrosse at the time, was a fabulous surprise.

I turned to Schnoo. "There's no way I'll ever let him go back to playing midfield. He's as good an any goalie I've ever seen."

Schnoo nodded and smiled. "It's not going to be easy, ya know. Courtenay really loves playing middie."

I found an ingenious way out of my predicament. I devised a plan whereby I'd always tell Servary that whatever year it was, it was his *last* year in the goal.

"Next year," I would lie, "I'm recruiting this great goalie. Just play out this season, Courtenay, and I promise you'll play midfield next year."

Attackman William "Bubbie" Bennett scoring against Roanoke. *(photo: Sid Brooks)*

O

The first game of the year against Roanoke College, played at Morgan, was disastrous. They beat the Bears 18 to 12. Wayne was the only player who had a decent game. Afterwards, Wayne told me, "We're not in shape, Coach. We need to run more." Some of the other players overheard this, and were pissed off.

The next day at practice when Wayne arrived, the peeved players started singing, "Superstar, Superstar, who in the hell does Wayne think he are?"

But Wayne took it in stride. He laughed and retorted, "That's not grammatically correct. You've got a singular subject and a plural verb."

O

A couple of concerned players were huddled with Poopie at the far end of the practice field. One of them was defenseman John Bacon who told Poopie, "God, I hate to tell the coach this, but I just got my grades and I think I'm academically ineligible."

"We can't stand to lose any more players," whispered Poopie. "You've got to get you a new identity and a high GPA (grade point average). Go tell Coach that you changed your name."

"Right," said Bacon. "I'll change it to one of those Muslim or African names that are pretty popular on campus. Got to be a few with the same name, and one of them's got to have a GPA high enough to be eligible. That's who I'll be."

"I can dig it," interrupted Poopie, "but, if you happen to make All-American or get mentioned in the newspapers, you can use your 'slave' name. We'll just tell Chip it's kind of a black thing. He won't understand it, but he'll believe it."

O

John Bacon was born in east Baltimore near Johns Hopkins Hospital. When his parents divorced, he was eight years old. After the divorce, he moved with his mother to Brooklyn, New York to stay with relatives. He spent his summers in Virginia with his uncle in an attempt to keep him out of the trouble he was getting into on the streets of Brooklyn.

In Brooklyn, John grew up among large Jewish and Hispanic populations. An old man named Fleischman who owned a grocery store befriended him. John liked the Jews. He worked for them on their Sabbath weekends when they couldn't touch anything electrical. For money, Bacon would press elevators, turn on lights, move cars, and things like that.

Mr. Fleischman taught John how to play baseball. Fleischman told John about how he would have played for the Yankees in the '30s except that there was a quota for Jews, and it had already been met. It didn't matter that he was better than some of the existing players; only that he was a Jew. He was like a step-dad to John, bringing him clothes and treating him like his own. (While John was also fond of Fleischman, this fondness didn't preclude him from screwing Fleischman's daughter during Christmas vacation of his freshman year.)

When John returned from Virginia at the end of the summer of his thirteenth year, his mother told him she had a surprise. She drove right past their home in Brooklyn all the way to Suffolk County where she showed him their new house. His mom had hit "the number" and bought them a house on Long Island. She took a job near their home at the state hospital, and John attended North Junior High where he learned to play lacrosse, football, and basketball.

Bacon attended high school at Brentwood High and played J.V. football his first year. At that time, Brentwood was 95 percent white.

John played so well at the J.V. level that he was promoted to the varsity. However, there were very strict rules about using a player in J.V. and varsity games late in the season. So John changed his name to Dino Sarmiento (Bacon thought he looked like his Italian schoolmates) and played on the varsity for two games. By his junior year, he was a varsity wrestler and was playing varsity football and lacrosse. In his senior year, John made All-Suffolk County in football as a center and linebacker, and he was also selected All-Long Island in lacrosse on defense.

At Brentwood High, John was a star athlete and good student. One day his mother came home and told him with pride, "No one takes my money at the market, the cleaners, or anywhere else. Everyone thinks of you as a local sports hero."

Bacon was a much sought-after football recruit, and a number of colleges, including Syracuse, Maryland, Michigan, and Hofstra, pursued him. Interestingly enough, most of the recruiting was not for lacrosse.

John was greatly influenced during this period by the Black Power movement, and listened to a couple of the black teachers at

Brentwood who advised him, "Go to a historically black college. Don't play for the white man. He'll use you up. You won't get a degree, and they'll mess with your head." So John decided to go to Morgan State.

John arrived at Morgan with what was probably the school's last great football recruiting class. All twenty recruits that year were All-State players from throughout the U.S., and at least three were first-team high school All-Americans. John's athletic career at Morgan started out poorly. He arrived two weeks late for summer football practice, showing up in a Corvette, and practiced with white football shoes. Coach Phillips, the line coach, pulled him aside and said, "We don't wear them shoes down here, champ; and take that fancy car home."

John "copped an attitude" immediately. He didn't get along with Coach Banks or any of the coaching assistants. He missed his buddies from Long Island. They had kept in touch, and he was surprised to hear how so many of them, while not even being starters at major schools, had finagled new cars in the recruitment process. They also told him they were getting money and were screwing lots of gorgeous white women. Even if they didn't play in a game, there was an envelope with at least $50 waiting for them when the game was over. And if they played well, it could be worth from $200 to $1,000 a game.

○

At Morgan, players had to worry about losing their scholarships in the spring if they didn't play well during the fall. Sometimes they even lost their rooms. Everyone always thought it was an administrative foul-up when it happened, but John didn't believe it. He was also shocked at the quality of equipment at Morgan. It didn't even hold a candle to the equipment at his high school.

Bacon became disenchanted. He had come to Morgan thinking it would be a black Utopia. Instead, he found coaches who seemed indifferent, no training table stocked with great food, second-rate equipment, no whirlpool, and a trainer who wouldn't tape your ankles if he didn't like you. "So much for Black Power," he wrote home.

For the Grambling game, even though John made the traveling squad, he knew he wouldn't see any action. So he didn't even wear his uniform or appear on the sidelines. Instead, he sat in the stands and drank liquor. At halftime, surprisingly, Coach Banks called for him. An assistant coach had to go into the stands and help John down. He was so blitzed he could barely walk.

○

The first Urban League game was the only time Morgan ever beat Grambling. Raymond Chester starred offensively and defensively, and it was believed this game was the reason he later became a first-round pro-draft pick. Morgan won the game 9 to 7 with a heartstopping, four-down goal-line stand. They had stopped Grambling a few minutes earlier when the Grambling place-kicker missed a field goal.

○

In 1970, John Bacon, Miles Harrison Jr., and some other protesters were planning to take over the Administration Building. They had chains that they were going to wrap all around the building and themselves. Similar demonstrations were taking place elsewhere among black colleges. But someone called President Jenkins and alerted him. At six a.m. when everyone snuck over to the Administration Building, they found it surrounded by city police and security personnel.

Later that week, at another protest march, students were poised on the bridge that ran overtop of Cold Spring Lane, which split the campus in half. They were "bombing" cars by throwing rocks and bottles from the bridge. John Bacon took hold of half a cinder block and threw it down on a passing Cadillac. It bounced off the hood of the Cadillac and back up onto the bridge, narrowly missing John's head. From that day on, Bacon only wanted to own a Cadillac.

By his second year, Coach Banks had pulled Bacon's scholarship. He was upset that John had gotten married and had a child while at Morgan. After the scholarship was revoked, Bacon wrote the head coach at the University of Maryland requesting a scholarship/transfer there, but found that he wouldn't be eligible right away. So he dropped out of school for a while, later returning and coming out for the 1971 lacrosse team. He was a good player, but two weeks into practice he quit. He needed to work nights to feed his family.

○

Dave Raymond was missing for the second game of the season against Wooster College, and I was surprised. Although there were always some players who missed practice and even an occasional game, I was shocked that a dedicated player like Dave was AWOL. I mentioned it to Poopie who said he'd take care of it.

It turned out Dave had gone back to New York. He was homesick and wondered if he had made a mistake coming to Morgan. He was considering a transfer to Adelphi University.

O

Schnoo Snyder coached defense part-time, showing up for practices a dozen or so times a season (and at most games), and especially when Pimlico Race Track was in session. He worked various jobs as a claims adjuster and title searcher. Every time he appeared at practice or a game, he proved disruptive, yet I, still in awe of his lacrosse ability from high school and college, let him have his way.

Once during a rare full-field scrimmage at Morgan State (the Bears seldom had over 20 players at any one time show up for practice), Snyder stopped play to chastise our only other goalie, Ed "Monk" Parker. (Bruce Herling had been injured.)

Snyder, who had arrived late, was unaware that we were in the middle of practicing clearing the ball after a shot on goal that began with a "loose ball." Parker was instructed not to catch our shots on goal, but to bat them away toward our defensemen so that they could scoop them up and begin clearing in that manner.

"Parker," Schnoo screamed, "you are the worst goalie I've ever seen; and I've seen them all!"

I tried to interrupt Schnoo and explain the drill, but he roared on. He chastised Monk for over three minutes. Finally, Monk broke.

"You take the damn stick, Mr. Big Time!" Monk screamed at Snyder. "I'm finished." And he ran off.

He didn't return for two weeks and was never the same afterwards. Whenever Snyder showed up, Monk would just drop his equipment and walk off the field.

O

The team was preparing to leave for an away game at Villanova in Philadelphia. I complained to Athletic Director Banks about how the bus had broken down a couple of times, causing delays and almost resulting in the forfeiture of games.

"Sibman, this is the bus line we're sticking with. We only use black-owned-and-operated buses. That's our philosophy here at Morgan."

Apprehensively, I climbed on board the bus noticing Oliver Chambers in the front seat with two nasal inhalers stuck up his nose.

Schnoo was in the back of the bus harmonizing with Wayne and several players. He liked to believe that he had "soul" and could relate to young black adults. (Schnoo could be a bit delusional.) They were doing some rhyming to a song called "The Signifying Monkey." Schnoo interrupted and told the players that a new fad called "rapping," which was growing in California, was headed east. He explained that a black poet named Leroy Jones had been the first to perform poetry with music in the background. Jones then moved to spouting the poetry to the beat of the music, starting the rapping fad.

"This is going to be the next big music rage," Schnoo speculated.

Afterwards, Schnoo walked up to the front of the bus.

"It'll never be popular," said Wayne. "Old Schnoo, he don't know what he's talking about. Now he's an expert on black music? He's seriously crazy."

Suddenly, the bus driver, "Pops," pulled over to the side of the road and stopped. When I asked him what was wrong, Pops yelled out, "We're not going anywhere until some thief returns my *Harold Melvin and the Blue Notes* tape."

Somebody had stolen it and Pops was determined to stay put until the state police arrived. For 15 minutes, I walked up and down the aisle of the bus trying to locate the tape. I threatened the players with being late for the game and the possibility of having to forfeit. Miraculously, the tape appeared on my seat, and the team was able to proceed to the game.

Arriving late, the team hustled off the bus and went out immediately to warm up and practice. A player from the other team walked by and called Danny Bell a "nigger." Danny punched the guy. One of the referees saw the incident and told me that Bell couldn't play in the game as a result.

I quickly called the team together. "You don't lose control," I began. "You don't show your emotions to the other team. Anybody who can't control his emotions is not going to play for me. What happened to Danny is an example, but I'm going to let it slide. However, if it happens again, Danny, you're off the team.

We will not let any opponent take us out of our game by calling us names."

Meanwhile, fearful that Raymond would leave Morgan again, Poopie spent a lot of time talking to Dave during the game, giving him encouragement about his game style and his commitment to the team.

In the latter part of the Villanova contest, Wayne began dominating and seemed to be able to score at will. After the game, Danny Bell asked him, "How do you do it? I heard you being called 'nigger' and 'boy' a thousand times in the first three quarters."

"Every time I scored a goal," said Wayne, "or knocked a player down, or got an assist, or made a great play, I would tell the other guy, 'That's how a nigger does it, that's how a boy scores.' Finally, they realized that there ain't no sense in inflaming me anymore; so near the end of the third quarter they just kept their damn mouths shut!"

○

At Poopie's apartment near Mondawmin Shopping Center, a discussion was underway about how Schnoo continued to scream and yell at everyone during the game, and then wanted to be their buddy afterwards. The players were getting fed up with it, and plotted revenge.

"I've got an idea," said Dickie Hall. "We'll make our 'statement' to Schnoo at the away game up in New York, at Hofstra."

The pregame get-togethers at Poopie's were dubbed "sessions." It became a ritual for some to get high and bond before every game.

In the corner of Poopie's living room, Dave Raymond sat with Millie.

After Millie left Poopie's, Dave talked about moving out of his dorm and into an apartment. He explained that too many girls were dropping by. He couldn't study, and Millie was getting suspicious.

"Are you *still* homesick, Dave?" asked Poopie.

"A little," confessed Raymond.

○

Morgan State was playing against St. Mary's College from southern Maryland, and more fans were in attendance at the game than any other that spring. Right before the game began, the play-ers were surprised to see the cheerleading squad, in uniform, arriv-ing on the field. Gerald Nesbit, an attackman, was shocked. "Wow, we must have arrived. We actually have cheerleaders."

They didn't realize that Millie, the head cheerleader, brought the cheerleading squad to the game so that she could be around Dave Raymond.

Morgan's cheerleading squad with Millie Yates. (second from right).

During the game, a blonde with a mini-skirt came walking across the field. It was my wife. She sat on the bench with the players.

In the third quarter, I noticed that one of the midfield units was in too long. (A midfield could only run for about two or three minutes before tiring, since his position required extensive sprint-ing up and down the field for the entire game.) I kept calling for the next midfield unit to go in, but they weren't responding. Five minutes elapsed and the tongues of the on-field midfielders were hanging out.

Seeing my mounting distress, my wife came up to me and said, "I don't think they're going in until they're finished singing."

On the bench, the first midfield unit of Wayne, Holley, and Pritchett were singing "I Want To Take You Higher."

When the game ended, one of St. Mary's assistant coaches, never even surmising that maybe the blonde was my wife, walked up to me and asked, "Which one of your players is the blonde married to?"

I pointed to the biggest and blackest player walking by and whispered, "Him!"

○

After the game, in the locker room, several older and larger players dragged Oliver Chambers and some other teammates into the showers, again threatening to rape them. The white players, Courtenay and Andi, watched in horror. And for good reason. They had been, at that moment, discussing the size of Cherry's and Ashe's cocks.

○

Oliver Chambers was Morgan's fastest midfielder. He was also a great shoplifter. Oliver would go into the A & P and Grand Union supermarkets after taking orders from some of the players for special cuts of meats. One time he asked Andi if his mother needed any special meats for Passover. Andi checked with his mother and found that she did need a certain cut of brisket. After Oliver sold the brisket to Andi at a very reduced price, Andi's mother claimed it wasn't lean enough, so Oliver returned to the supermarket and stole a leaner cut.

Oliver used to joke that the grocery stores would need former Olympic sprinter Bob Hayes as a security guard if they wanted to catch him.

○

In a return grudge match against BPI at Morgan, it appeared that certain BPI players' strategy was to upset the Ten Bears by calling them "niggers." Morgan had beaten them the year before in a controversial game, 8 to 7. So when they went out onto the field, the BPI players kept saying, "I've got Nigger Number Five, I've got Nigger Number Thirteen . . ." The Morgan starters were livid, but I told them to maintain their composure.

I asked the BPI coach to stop the name-calling, but he would only comment, "It's outta my hands."

The BPI players were even hassling the whites. One player called Andi an albino, and he became incensed. He started yelling and cursing as defenseman Tony Bullock tried to calm him down.

"It ain't that bad, Andi. The sun ain't even out."

The players respected my wishes that they not lose control over the racial slurs. Morgan lost the game after a close first half, 12 to 6. When the game ended, I told the guys, "Okay, the game's over. I have no control over you, anymore."

The BPI team celebrated and dawdled on the field before leaving. The Morgan players immediately positioned themselves at the top of the steps of the stadium. As BPI's team walked up the steps, the Bears were standing there with some additional football player friends waiting to "discuss" the "nigger" comments.

Once the "discussions" began, the BPI coach and his captains ran over to me to beg for help. I was talking to Tiger Davis at the time.

When the BPI coach and captains asked, then begged, me to intervene, I said, "It's out of my hands." And after they begged harder, I asked Tiger to mediate a settlement.

Tiger put his arm around the shoulder of the BPI coach and said, "Don't worry about it, brother, you have a right to hate. But, don't be uptight. The sting is worse than the bite, brother. I'm available for sensitivity training before you leave. But, of course, at a price . . ."

○

Morgan Holley was a great team player, always urging the guys on, and was very supportive if a player made a mistake.

Holley lived in an apartment near Bubbie's home by Memorial Stadium and City College. When he and Bubbie would go home after practice, they'd sit on the steps in front of Holley's apartment building, and Holley would talk about Vietnam. One time Holley drew a picture of himself and several friends in a foxhole and showed it to Bubbie. It wasn't artistic, but it was tough for Bubbie to take his eyes off of it. Holley had seen a lot of his friends killed in Vietnam. He told Bubbie about staying in a foxhole for days and nights, and would expand upon the frivolity of war.

Since Holley and Poopie were both vets, it was inevitable that they would develop a relationship, even though Holley was more of an introvert and Poopie was the gregarious sort.

○

After the games and practices, most of the players would go to Poopie's apartment and replay the game and talk about funny things that had happened. Some would get high and/or drink. This helped develop great camaraderie among the players.

However, some guys were still cautious in the group. John Bacon was always leery of Cherry. He was afraid that if he got high, Cherry was liable to mess with him. He didn't realize that when Cherry got high, he was calm and very mellow.

Dickie Hall could never figure Cherry out, and finally gave up trying. Although Dickie became a social acquaintance of Cherry's in college, he still could not take being picked on by him. One night Poopie, Dickie, and Cherry went to a party together. Stanley began picking on Dickie as soon as they arrived, and Dickie decided that enough was enough. He pulled out a gun and threatened to shoot Cherry if he didn't lay off. After that, Stanley never bothered Dickie again.

○

Dickie joined ROTC and was commissioned a second lieutenant in the Army for military intelligence. In 1972, Dickie was used in an ad in the *ROTC Magazine* and, as a result, Morgan State gave him a partial-tuition scholarship.

He was a member of an elite core within ROTC called the "Watson Rangers," a Special-Forces-like group. They did survival-type exercises. It was like a private fraternity.

○

In a game at Randolph Macon College in Virginia played on a field by the railroad tracks, the players were intimidated by the rowdy fans and what we considered biased Southern refereeing. The fans were extremely boisterous and were throwing beer cans and rocks throughout the game. The local referees were prejudiced in their calls, obviously favoring the Randolph Macon team. It was so upsetting that former goalie, now midfielder, Bruce Herling, actually dove angrily into the crowd after some of the name-calling.

In spite of the provocations and with a five-goal lead going into the last quarter, we figured we had a major upset. Randolph

Macon was a highly ranked team. Wayne had won almost every face-off, but for the last fifteen minutes of the fourth quarter, every penalty went against Morgan, and we lost 16 to 15.

On the way back from the game, the guys were pissed off over the loss and the fan abuse. Oliver Chambers, who was drinking a can of beer that he had smuggled onto the bus, threw the beer can out of the window. A Virginia state trooper saw it and pulled the bus over. I had to do some real sweet-talking to keep the whole team from going to jail, especially since Pops, the bus driver, tried to convince the trooper to arrest everyone. Pissed that Pops had turned on the team, Chambers permanently "borrowed" his *Harold Melvin and the Blue Notes* tape.

○

Since the budget cycle was in full swing in mid-spring, I was presenting to Earl Banks in the athletic office, again trying to get additional funds for the players for next season. "Most of the sticks are broken," I whined. But, as usual, my request was denied until I alluded to a trip across campus to the president's office.

Banks asked me if I was aware of any of my players abusing drugs, because he had heard some rumors.

"Absolutely not!" I roared. "I can tell. That's the field I'm in. Christ, Coach Banks, I run the Drug Abuse Administration. Nothing like that's happening on my team!"

I was in a quandary. Drug use and abuse were rampant on American campuses, and as much as I didn't want to acknowledge it, I knew many of my players were using. To what degree, I wasn't sure. So I adopted the same philosophy I had used with friends and acquaintances—I would not bring up my suspicions unless an individual came to me for help.

○

A couple of the players were getting high at Poopie's, smoking marijuana. Tiger Davis dropped by and chastised them about the negative effects of "reefer" on the black community.

"This reefer ain't no good," said Tiger. "You've got to come out of this shit. It's counter-revolutionary. It's not keeping the faith."

"Hey, this is the real world," said Poopie. "We feel better high."

But then Tiger would retort, "Everything has its price, but

this shit ain't got any place in high struggles."

"Hey man . . ." interrupted Poopie, ready to rebut. But then he drifted off.

○

Raymond missed two days of practice. He had gone home again. I called his parents, and they told me that while Dave was a little homesick, he was getting better and would meet the team at Hofstra on Long Island for the next game. The Raymonds lived near Hofstra in Hempstead, Long Island.

The night before the Hofstra game, Dave Raymond came by the dorm where Morgan's lacrosse team was staying. He convinced about 20 players to sneak out and go to a party down the street from Hofstra. Tony Bullock persuaded a handful of borderline players not to go. "If Chip finds out, we won't play or get our per diem."

Before or after an away game, I doled out money from the Athletic Department to the players. The money was for food or incidentals, and amounted to around six dollars per player. However, I would allocate higher or lower sums depending on how well or poorly a player performed. I gave out the money in an envelope, telling the better players, "Here, you got $10 because you played well. Don't tell anyone what you received." To the others I said, "This is all the per diem that the A.D. allotted."

Tony, an overweight but agile defenseman, usually received only three dollars, but somehow ended up with more food and five pounds heavier after each trip.

Bullock watched forlornly from the dorm window as 20 of his teammates walked down the street in Hempstead. (A cop car drove by the guys very slowly and trailed the players several blocks before leaving.)

○

Surprisingly, Morgan played very well against the highly ranked and talented Hofstra team. They were bewildered by our strategy and tenacity. At halftime, with the game tied at 4 to 4, the referee came into the Morgan locker room to check for illegal sticks. He put a ball in every stick to check the pocket depth. This was unheard of. The top-ten, Division I, nationally-ranked Hofstra team couldn't believe Morgan's players' stickwork and had complained to the refs. All the sticks checked out.

We had never played on an Astroturf field before, and were amazed at the bounce-passes of the Hofstra players. Their apparent strategy was to cover Wayne Jackson with several players. This left Daryl Echols open, and he had a great game; but Morgan lost 10 to 6. Wayne smartly attempted to dump the ball off, but the offensive players somehow couldn't catch his passes.

Because Hofstra's field was artificial, we had to wear special shoes borrowed from our opponent. The shoes made the players' feet sore, which also contributed to the loss.

Schnoo and I were discussing what happened in the second half. "I can't figure it out," said Schnoo. "I thought we were ready for that same zone that they threw up against us last year. Why don't we just ask their coach what they did?"

"We can't do that," I said. "Nobody does that. You never ask the strategy of an opposing coach. I mean, we're coaches, aren't we? Shouldn't we be able to analyze what happened?"

"I don't think so," replied Schnoo. "Why don't we just ask him?"

"All right then."

We went over to the Hofstra locker room. "Well, what did you do?" I asked the coach. "I mean, it looked like a normal zone. Why couldn't we score?"

Hofstra's coach was Howdy Meyers, a 70-year-old man who was a legendary strategist. "Look, we know how good Wayne is; so, not only did we use our normal zone, but we formed a box and one. We had an extra player on Wayne the whole time, besides playing zone defense."

Schnoo and I looked at each other, shaking our heads as we walked back to the visiting team's dressing room.

"There's something else," I said. "Wayne told me that the New York players, like from Hofstra and Adelphi, aren't intimidated by Morgan . . . They're not afraid of blacks!"

"Of course not," said Schnoo, "they're from New York!"

○

The players were climbing onto the bus back to Baltimore, and a few of them, including Dickie Hall, told me that they had permission to stay in New York and return the next night.

"Who gave you permission?" I asked.

"Our parents," said Hall.

"Do you have notes?" I asked.

"Notes? You mean from our parents?" countered Hall.

"Yeah."

"Christ, you're insensitive, Chip. Most black kids either have illiterate parents, single parents, or don't know their parents. What's wrong with you?"

"I'm sorry," I responded, "but you guys gotta be back by Monday. I'm responsible."

As the players began to leave, I realized I'd been hoodwinked and screamed, "Then who the hell gave you permission?!"

Hall and Bacon took Schnoo aside. In a conspiratorial tone, Hall said, "Hey Schnoo, my man, convince Chip to let us stay in New York. Tell him you'll take responsibility. If you help us out, we'll take you with us and drop you at Belmont."

Schnoo wasn't about to turn down a free ride to the racetrack, so he went along.

I boarded the bus and took the remaining team back home.

Schnoo and the others headed in the direction of New York City. Suddenly, the players took a detour into Bedford-Stuyvesant, an extremely rough area, especially if one is white, and pushed Schnoo out of the car. They screamed, "Nigger," honked the horn several times loudly, and then sped away.

○

After practice, Danny Bell warned Bubbie that Cherry was looking to smack him around and that the best thing for him to do was to hide. Danny convinced Bubbie to squeeze into a gym locker. "I'll close and lock it to save you from Cherry," promised Bell, winking at the other players close by.

But Cherry never showed up. The players forgot about Bubbie and left to go home. While they were standing at the bus stop, they realized that Bubbie was still in the locker. Danny ran back and let him out. Bubbie was livid, but Danny told him, "Cherry was hanging around outside, hiding; so we all left, hoping he'd go away."

○

As the "Free Ochiki" movement continued to grow, prison officials, fearful of Ochiki's leadership ability, threw him and several other men into a punishment cell. They were left naked and without bedding for 35 days, surviving on stale sandwiches.

○

Interestingly, Morgan's ascent in lacrosse came about during the metamorphosis of the modern lacrosse stick. Beginning in the seventies, the lacrosse stick's design went from a one-piece stick and curve made of wood with leather and gut webbing to a metal/aluminum alloy shaft with a heavy plastic shell and mesh webbing. This transformation dramatically altered the game. The previous weight of the stick and curvature of the head had made dexterous stickwork only for a talented few; but now even the novice could, after a few weeks, handle the lacrosse stick with the aplomb of a skilled veteran. Players could throw the ball longer with more accuracy, and cradle and dodge without the fear of dropping the ball. Not only did the feel and sight of the game change, the sound level of the checking was exaggerated. Wood on wood or wood on body changed to wood on metal and metal on plastic as body armor was also replaced and lengthened. Plastic shoulder and armpads were added, or replaced heavily padded elbow pads. The players were bigger, faster, and stronger than in previous eras, and the noise from the game grew more rhythmic, brutal, and frightening.

○

Cherry returned to play after recovering from his back operation. I tried to discourage him by explaining that he could reinjure his back and that it could affect his future pro football career. Since Cherry had only one more year of eligibility to play college ball, I didn't want to see him get injured before the football season.

"Well, Coach," said Stanley, "I'm comin' back for two reasons. One, Syracuse has two guys who are All-American football players, and I want to see how tough they are. Second, I'm still trying to figure out why you helped me out, you being white and all that. I still don't get it."

○

During pregame warmups, the Morgan players watched hypnotically as Syracuse's Native American Indians whipped the ball around adroitly, handling the stick as if it were an extension of their hands.

Right before the game, Cherry and Wayne were walking down the steps into Hughes Stadium eating enormous cold cut submarines.

When the game began, the first shot hit the goal and knocked it over. Courtenay called a time-out and yelled, "That's it! I'm out of here. I want to play midfield. I'm going to get killed!"

I reassured him, telling Courtenay I'd pay for all doctor or emergency room visits resulting from the Syracuse shooters.

This first time that Morgan played the Native-American-dominated Syracuse lacrosse team, there was a major clash of cultures. Some called it the "Ultimate Affirmative Action Bowl." The Indian players called the blacks "wool heads and Brillo tops," while the Morgan blacks referred to the Indians as "Spics, Tonto, and Crazy Horse."

Led by legendary Canadian box lacrosse stars Freeman Bucktooth and the Hill Brothers (Ron and Oliver), the Syracuse Native Americans could twirl their sticks like batons. They were all from the Onondaga Reservation. To protect their arms, which were beaten upon more in their box lacrosse venue, the Indians rolled copies of *Life* magazine around their biceps and lower arms and secured them with duct tape. (Some Morgan players adopted this protective device when the school couldn't afford the plastic armguards.)

During the game, the weather fluctuated astoundingly—from snow to sleet to rain to bright sunshine. The checking, both stick and body, the language of name-calling, grunts, and dialects, and the field game sounds of cleated and uncleated shoes on the hard field and sloshing about on the muddy sidelines were unique to the usual soundtrack of Morgan's games.

Freeman Bucktooth wore very ragged gloves. He would wind up from the midfield line and fire the ball so fast and hard that if his aim was accurate, he usually scored. Everyone moved out of the way when Bucktooth cranked up to shoot the ball. He had long coal-black hair that swirled in the wind from underneath his helmet.

Courtenay was yelling at the midfielders and defensemen, "Get in front of his shot! Block his shot!" But the guys would only scream back, "No way! Hell if I am! That's your job, Courtenay!"

Andi was guarding Oliver Hill and, at one point, pushed him illegally out-of-bounds. "Son, you don't want to do that," Oliver said matter-of-factly, but Andi knew and respected the menacing tone of the soft voice. So he ambled over to Bacon and whispered, "J.B., you guard the chief."

Coach Chip Silverman in the snow on the sidelines during the Syracuse game.
(Photo: Martin W. Denker)

Cherry was like a wild man that day. Joe Erhman, who was an All-American lineman and later played for the Baltimore Colts, was on that Syracuse team along with Tommy Myers, who later played for the New Orleans Saints. Stanley went around trying to hit them and anyone else in his way. It was like two trains colliding when he and Erhman ran into each other.

During the third quarter, Cherry got upset with Bacon over a miscommunication that resulted in a goal, and they began yelling at each other, then fighting. They had to be separated by Wayne. After the game, John sat naked on a bench in the dressing room. All of a sudden Cherry came up from behind and started choking him.

"Thought I forgot, huh?" he whispered. Poopie and Holley ran over to restrain Stanley, but as soon as that happened Cherry started laughing.

The game, won by Syracuse 16 to 13, was bloody and aggressively played since there was obviously an inherent dislike between the two teams. Wayne played exceptionally, and at the end of the game, the Syracuse coach sang his praises, exclaiming that Wayne reminded him of the great Jim Brown.

A couple of the players, Bubbie and Danny Bell, overheard the coach's compliment, and Bubbie said, "Yeah, Chip's always telling us that if we play good, we can be like Jim Brown."

Bell added, "Right on. We can fuck movie stars and hang out at the Playboy Mansion."

○

"Chip," Bubbie asked later, "how good was Jim Brown?"

"A lot of people considered him the greatest of all time," I said. "I happened to have been in that crowd of about 6,500 at Hopkins' Homewood Field back in 1957; although, today there are about 200,000 people who swear they saw that North-South All-Star Game. Anyhow, Brown was spectacular, probably putting on one of the greatest individual performances in the history of the North-South Games. The North team won easily 14 to 10. Brown controlled every face-off he was involved in. He scored five goals, assisted on two, and his speed and stickwork were amazing. Not only that, when guys tried to check him and knock him down, they only succeeded in bouncing off Brown's massive body. They were flying every which way but Sunday. He was unstoppable and only played half of the game."

My discussions about Brown over the years always proved motivational and inspirational to the players.

○

Attorney William M. Kunstler's motion for a speedy trial for H. Rap Brown was denied. Howard County Judge James MacGill ruled that New York City had jurisdiction over where Brown could be tried first. Brown was awaiting trial in Rikers Island, the New York detention facility.

SUMMER 1972

I sat in the kitchen of my house staring in disbelief at the newspaper. I was heartbroken. My mentor, "The Dean," Frank A. DeCosta Sr., had died suddenly of a heart attack. The dean's death caught everyone by surprise. As I found out later from Beautine DeCosta, her husband had been ill for quite sometime but had kept it to himself. He was never one to complain.

While Dr. DeCosta appeared to be a living contradiction—he had been involved in an advisory capacity during the Montgomery bus boycott and other civil rights movements, but his politics were steeped in the genteel conservatism of his hometown of Charleston, South Carolina—he was a man of purpose and high integrity, and had an intense belief in his abilities. And he truly believed that one day civil rights would prevail.

○

With the help of Coach Banks, I was able to get Wayne, Bell, Cherry, Andi, and John Bacon summer jobs as counselors at Camp Concern, a summer day camp for kids sponsored by the Federal Anti-Poverty Program.

Buses picked up 800 kids between seven and seventeen years old in east Baltimore every weekday and took them to the Naval base in Bainbridge, Maryland or the Army facility at Fort Meade. There were police chalk marks on the street and drunks passed out on the sidewalks every morning as they waited for the buses.

I thought it would be good for the guys to work with Camp Concern. They'd be helping out disadvantaged kids while also picking up some extra money. However, if I had known the kind of pranks they'd pull, I might have reconsidered recommending them as counselors.

Andi and John Bacon were assigned to the Bainbridge base. While there, Andi fell in love with a married girl whose husband worked summers in California (where he attended U.C.L.A. on a football scholarship). Bacon protected Andi by trying to keep the husband's friends from discovering the tryst.

In storehouses at Bainbridge there were loads of used furniture. Bacon made "arrangements" to sell it to surplus dealers he knew in New York.

Wayne, Cherry, and Danny Bell worked at the other Camp Concern facility at Fort Meade where they were lifeguards. One day, Wayne saved a young boy from drowning. After he removed the victim from the pool and resuscitated him, he carried the boy over to the nurse's station, a small building with a bed, hospital supplies, and, Wayne hoped, a nurse. But Wayne could not pry the door open to the station and had to break it down. When he got inside, still carrying the boy in his arms, he found Danny Bell and Stanley sitting on the bed with two coeds from Morgan State performing oral sex.

"Get off the bed!" screamed Wayne.

"Not till we're finished," said Cherry. "Then you can use it with the boy," he added, jokingly. That's when the nurse arrived and freaked out.

CHAPTER 7

WHUPPIN'S

FALL 1972

As fall approached, I was busy trying to recruit new members for the team while also trying to keep the older players out of academic trouble.

I was recruiting a young Essex Community College student named Billy Johns, who told me he would rather work for the Baltimore County Fire Department than continue his education. Trying to convince him that getting the Other-Race Grant to play lacrosse at Morgan would be a better idea, I was showing Billy around campus when we met three other new recruits: Dink Brown, Tyrone Scott, and Jerna Jacques. At first blush, they impressed me in a negative way: out of control, loud, and too playful. A generation of nihilists. In that instant, I realized what a challenge it would be to keep them eligible, to keep them alive, and to keep the older players from beating them up.

○

In the gym in the Hill Field House, I was attempting to persuade basketball seven-footer, Marvin Webster, to go out for lacrosse.

"I'll put you on the crease in front of the goal, and nobody will stop you," I said.

Nat Frazier, the new basketball coach, overheard the comment. He told me not to come near his players, and ordered me out of the gym.

○

Andi and five other white radicals attempted to form a White Student Union at the urging of a white professor who was once a member of the Dutch Resistance in World War II. Courtenay refused to join since he wasn't political and was also rebuilding a motorcycle in his spare time so that he could commute from the farm faster. He had moved back to his old neighbors' 145-acre farm where he was living in the barn belonging to the two elderly brothers.

To express his solidarity with their cause, Andi dropped his Other-Race Grant and decided to pay for school. He felt guilty about receiving the "free ride" to Morgan after Tony Bullock jokingly called him a mercenary. Dropping the grant was a dumb move since Andi didn't have a job to pay for college.

Because he was a very reliable defenseman, I got Andi a partial athletic scholarship after I agreed with Banks' request to use my salary to purchase new sticks. (This was the first year I received a coaching salary, $1,500, but I never saw a dime. Amazingly, I never considered requesting a salary or a higher salary. Being a head collegiate lacrosse coach and contemplating the potential of what the Ten Bears could attain was rewarding enough. It was almost intoxicating.) Andi didn't refuse the partial scholarship because it was based on athletic ability and not the color of his skin.

The informal White Student Union met with an outspoken member of the Morgan Student Government, who had written an editorial in the school paper espousing that Morgan should be *all* black. He discouraged Andi and his group. "If you want to live to see the second semester, I suggest you call off your quest!"

○

Poopie was entertaining Holley in his apartment. They were discussing Vietnam and how the streets and the city of Baltimore were as dangerous as 'Nam was.

"At least the Viet Cong had a purpose," lamented Holley.

"Yeah," said Poopie, "I can dig it."

They heard some yelling and arguing next-door and walked closer to the wall to listen. There was always a hassle there, and Poopie told Holley, "There's a lot of serious heroin dealing going on out of this girl's apartment by her boyfriend. It's a sad state of affairs."

○

While Millie was a Morgan student, she also worked two jobs. She was a nutritionist at Good Samaritan Hospital in the afternoon, preparing food for all of the patients. (She also made lots of sandwiches for Dave and the rest of the lacrosse team.) Dave usually had Millie's car. He would pick her up from the hospital and take her to her late-night job with the telephone company where she was a directory assistance operator. Dave was always supposed to pick Millie up from work, but a lot of times he didn't show. He had other social obligations.

One afternoon, Dave was driving around in Millie's car with Cherry, Oliver Chambers, and Poopie. They were looking to pick up some alcoholic beverages to go with the marijuana they already had. It was Election Day. This was the wrong day to be looking for booze since Election Day was always "dry" in the state of Maryland. To make matters worse, they pulled up to two scroungy-looking guys on Harford Road and asked them if they knew where to buy alcohol.

"Look, we're undercover cops," the guys said. "Get lost."

But shortly after Dave had driven away, they were pulled over by the two cops. They had to get out of the car while the cops searched it and found an ounce of marijuana shoved under the front seat. The cops frisked everyone, placed them under arrest, and called a paddy wagon. Dave and the guys were taken to jail, and Millie's car was towed to the impound lot.

In the meantime, Millie waited at the bus stop near Good Samaritan Hospital for Dave to pick her up. After two hours, she missed her night job and went home, without a car. Her parents were livid.

Dave and the guys were kept in jail for six hours. They dubbed themselves "The Morgan Four," somehow convincing each other that they were political prisoners. Finally, they were released on their own recognizance. Dave retrieved the car and drove to Millie's to explain. She went ballistic and didn't believe anything he said. It wasn't the first time that Dave had left her stranded.

The guys hired Billy Murphy, a young, black, up-and-coming criminal attorney, to defend them. He charged $500. Because they were students and no one admitted to where the grass came from (Chambers had bought it), the prosecution had a tough case to prove. Since the police couldn't pin the ounce of marijuana on anyone, Murphy convinced the judge to drop the case "against these fine but misguided students."

Dave figured that Millie was going to kick him out after what had happened, but she was a very forgiving person, and she took him back.

○

At a court hearing in New York prior to the H. Rap Brown trial on attempted murder and robbery, Attorney Kunstler tried to prove that police detectives fabricated evidence and entrapped Brown.

In a rare occurrence, court officials allowed Brown to meet privately with Berkeley radical Angela Davis, who was on a cross-country tour aiding political prisoners.

Later, Davis met with the media and told them that Brown was being persecuted. She also said that based on the number of police who showed up at the bar, it appeared that Rap had been set up.

WINTER 1972-73

I was at my third USILA Conference when I met with Jack Emmer, the new head coach for Washington and Lee, a great team with a storied lacrosse tradition. Emmer decided to schedule the first game of the year against Morgan, probably figuring Washington and Lee should win easily as a result of our down year in '72. Obviously, many coaches felt that the '71 year, Morgan's first at the varsity level, was a fluke. And still, I could not get a game with William and Mary.

I discussed with Cookie Krongard, chairman of the "Little" All-American Selection Committee (Division II), how well Wayne Jackson played lacrosse. "Wayne plays a unique game. Many of the black players play a white-man's game, but Wayne doesn't. He plays his own game. He's a very fluid player, and he has brought a spin to the game that Earl Monroe uses in basketball."

At a team meeting, I announced the schedule, discussed how great Washington and Lee was, and again explained the difference between Division I and Division II colleges. "We're going to have to start practice earlier," I said. "It might be in the snow, and there'll be a lot of running. We're going to take teams by surprise, especially those who think our first year was a fluke."

After the meeting, several players hung back and spoke about their grades, and using Muslim names just in case they were ineligible. As usual, most of the players internalized their enthusiasm, but I could tell they were psyched.

O

Bubbie and several of the players were at a Morgan basketball game watching their old schoolmate, Marvin Webster, from Edmondson High. Marvin had gone from an average player to an outstanding collegiate performer. He'd become a dominant player; blocking shots, scoring, and rebounding.

The Bears were playing Bethune-Cookman, a college from Florida, and Marvin was able to block just about every shot. Mike Maddox, the team manager for the Bears, yelled out to Bubbie, "Marvin is erasing the boards. He's blocking shot after shot. He's unbelievable!"

"Yeah, he's erasing the boards all right," echoed Bubbie.

"He's a human eraser," Maddox added. And the nickname stuck.

SPRING 1973

On the bus ride to Lexington, Virginia, home of Washington and Lee University, Oliver Chambers confided to me that he was scared because Cherry and others were threatening to rape him when we arrived.

"I'm tired of your whining about this," I scolded him loudly. "Actually, when we get to W & L, I'm considering gangbanging you along with the other players." Everyone laughed, including Oliver.

Later, I noticed Oliver with the nasal inhalers in his nose again.

"What's wrong?" I asked.

"Sinusitis, Coach," said Oliver.

The other players snickered and made gestures indicating cocaine.

The same bus driver, Pops, stopped the bus. Another tape was missing. It took only a few minutes to get him driving again as Bubbie consoled Pops while I located the tape in the bathroom.

Bullock and some players went to see *Reefer Madness* at an old theater in Lexington, Virginia. During the film, Bullock gave a running discourse, entertaining the counterculture clique at Washington and Lee.

Later, Scott, Dink, and Jacques wanted to desecrate Robert E. Lee's gravesite and had to be restrained by several upperclassmen.

At two-thirty in the morning, the players and coaches were in the gym playing a basketball game. Schnoo and I were on opposing teams. The W & L coach, Jack Emmer, showed up smiling, believing the Morgan players were going to tire themselves out and not play well in the afternoon lacrosse game.

I tried to explain to Emmer that the lifestyle of my players was one where they went to bed late all the time.

○

In the cafeteria line at W & L, the Morgan players were loading up with lunch. They couldn't believe how good the fare was, and some of them filled up two or three trays with food.

Again, Coach Emmer was beaming brightly. He wondered how Morgan's team was going to be able to play. He told his assistants, "Not only will they be too heavy and sick in the stomach to run, but they were up playing basketball till four in the morning!"

The lacrosse contest was surprisingly close for three quarters. Emmer kept glaring at me, shaking his head, and calling out, "What's going on here? I thought you guys weren't any good."

At one point, Wayne scored a one-handed goal, and Emmer rushed over to me and said, "What are you doing?! This is embarrassing! What's going on?!" Then he winked.

Tied at nine towards the end of the third quarter, we fell apart. Washington and Lee won 17 to 10. Emmer congratulated our entire team.

On the return trip, I stood up on the bus and told the players, "I'm very proud of everybody, and I want to congratulate you all. And as a show of appreciation, we're all going to screw Oliver and the white kids!"

Everyone started laughing except for Oliver, Andi, Billy Johns, and Courtenay. Finally they realized it was just a joke, and nervously laughed along.

○

At Wayne Jackson's house, the younger black players, including Scott and Raymond, were listening to Wayne's advice. "Don't be scared! It's not just a white man's game and there's nothing to fear. Lacrosse is all sports in one, especially basketball. But you got to get serious. Practice at home. Don't just run and shoot. Slow down. Take your time and think. Don't worry about the pressure. I love it. Look at it as a great experience; traveling to and playing against white schools we'd never have a chance to attend."

○

Not satisfied with the team's endurance level and unable to use the snow-covered field for practice, I made the team run the streets near Morgan while I drove alongside of them. I detoured to pick up a late lunch at McDonald's and spotted Gerald Nesbit, an AWOL attackman, inside of the restaurant.

"Why aren't you at practice, Nez?" I asked.

"You hardly been playing me in any of the games," answered Nesbit. "I should get a shot, Coach."

"Get in the car and we'll talk about it."

I caught up to the players and began to eat a Big Mac. I made Nesbit steer the car while I ate, and we discussed his playing time. The car almost hit a few players running alongside.

○

John Bacon was working nights at the Central Police Garage while attending Morgan. He was no longer playing football or lacrosse. I called him at home one day. John had to juggle the phone while he held his infant son on his shoulder and scrambled eggs.

"John, we can get to the playoffs if you come back," I pleaded. "I need you to play crease defense."

His wife, Janet, overhearing the conversation, began screaming, "You're crazy! You need to graduate. You need to keep working. We got a baby!"

When John returned to the team (after I used Jewish guilt on him), he was not just overweight, but in poor condition. So I made him run all the time. He ran around the field during the first three games until he got in better shape.

When he arrived at practice, he noticed a pretty student named Barbria who seemed to be a lacrosse fan. They developed an instant infatuation. (Seven years later, John divorced his first wife and married Barbria.)

○

Their confidence boosted from our good showing in the W & L game, the Ten Bears realized they could compete against anyone. The '73 season went very well, and we started beating a lot of teams we had lost to in the past. Leonard Spicer, a transfer student and excellent lacrosse player from the University of Maryland, provided additional athletic prowess and leadership. Nothing could deter the team from trying to get to the Division II Tournament. We knew we had a good shot.

All-American Wayne Jackson dodging past a Boston College midfielder.

○

On the way to Frostburg State College in far Western Maryland, the brakes on the bus burned out. The team still managed to get to the game on time after another black-owned-and-operated bus miraculously appeared.

Before the game, I told defenseman Maurice Ashe to stay

with the Frostburg star scorer, Shady Lane, wherever he went. Ashe, who took things seriously and literally, followed Lane into the huddle and, at halftime, into the men's room. Ashe was big, dark, and muscular. He took Lane completely out of the game through intimidation.

Morgan was winning easily after three quarters. Some disgruntled Frostburg fans were milling around me and grabbing at my longer-than-usual hair. Bacon, Poopie, and Bell became incensed at this behavior and ran into the stands fighting with the guys who had grabbed my hair. The referees threw Bacon out of the game.

Also, for some reason, the Frostburg coach's girlfriend, who had been keeping game time, had disappeared. Nobody could locate her, and the fourth quarter dragged on for an hour. Morgan's big lead began to evaporate. The score got closer and closer. We finally won, but only because it started getting dark. The coach's girlfriend was eventually found sleeping in her car with the time clock beside her.

After the Frostburg game, Andi and Bullock were walking around campus and came upon a newly built planetarium. They walked in and looked up at the artificial universe. Bullock mistook a cockroach walking on the ceiling for a planet and Andi chided him.

"You should know a roach, Bullock," said Andi. "It's part of your cultural background."

Bullock retorted, "You mean like gefilte fish is to yours?"

Bullock was still pissed off at me for ignoring his strategy before the game. It seemed that Bullock had viewed a couple of movies on Zulu tribes and became mesmerized over how they attacked during wars against other tribes. One of their attacking methods was called "horns of the buffalo" where warriors attacked from the flanks and then drove straight into the middle. Bullock told me that this would be a good strategy against Frostburg. I, of course, had no clue what he was referring to and made him run extra laps.

○

The Quaker-founded Friends School was a private institution in north Baltimore City that had produced numerous high school graduates who had become college All-American lacrosse players. During the early seventies, several former Friends' players who had participated in lacrosse in college and returned to the

Baltimore area formed a club lacrosse team. Although not an offi-cial member of the U.S. Club Lacrosse Association, they scrim-maged club and collegiate teams located in the metropolitan area. Organized by the Friends School lacrosse coach, Tom Lamonica, they played home games at either Friends' athletic field or at Lamonica's farm in northwest Baltimore County. The players were all college graduates, many with graduate degrees, and all were successfully employed.

Lamonica invited Morgan to an annual series of exhibitions beginning in 1973, and since the Bears' campus was only a few miles east of Friends School, we welcomed the opportunity. Play-ing against the Friends alumni was an educational experience. Al-though Morgan was quicker and had more stamina, our opponents had skill and savvy acquired from years of lacrosse experience. While Morgan players had, at the most, three years of lacrosse experience before college, the Friends Club team players picked up their first stick in early grade school and averaged fifteen to twenty years each of playing the game.

The Friends Club had a black defenseman named Frank Bond, who not only excelled at lacrosse in high school, but was also a standout at Johns Hopkins University.

Most of the Bears were shocked to see a black player with Friends School lineage. Bond's appearance—dark, tall, and built like a heavyweight fighter—earned the immediate respect of Morgan's team. But after they heard him speak (Bond later be-came a TV newscaster) and saw his camaraderie with the other preppy Friends alumni, they pegged him as a wimp. They would soon learn how badly they had underestimated him.

"Did ya hear that smooth-talkin', rep-tie-wearin' punk speak?" asked Tyrone Scott. "I'm gonna mess him up every chance I get!"

Scott played attack and midfield during his freshman year, and he got his chance to go up against Bond that day.

Bond's gentlemanly demeanor took a backseat when he played lacrosse, and he gave Scott and several other players a "whuppin'."

When the game ended in darkness, tied 12 to 12, and the teams shook hands at midfield, Scott approached Bond. "You talk like Shakespeare, man, but you are one tough brother!"

With that, Bond took Scott and a couple other players aside and pointed out the mistakes that they were making, as well as a few tricks of the trade. (Unbeknownst to Scott and the freshmen, Bond had grown up in Edmondson Village and was a neighbor of Cherry and Jackson—until his family moved when he was twelve.)

O

I was so busy with my day job at the D.A.A. (Drug Abuse Administration) and coaching the lacrosse team, not to mention my new marriage, it often seemed I was living in my own world, insulated from the troubles of the world at large. But just in case I forgot that we were living in turbulent times, events had a way of reminding me.

After practice one day, Poopie, Holley, and Andi attended a huge antiwar rally being staged by three local schools: Morgan, Towson State University, and Johns Hopkins. The event, held near City Hall in Baltimore, was peaceful initially, but grew ugly after several volatile speeches and the sighting of a large police presence.

Some rocks and bottles were thrown, and it brought an immediate response: tear gas. The crowd began to disperse until they saw Holley and Poopie, former Vietnam vets, scooping up the canisters in their lacrosse sticks and heaving them back at the cops.

Several other vets were in the crowd, and they proceeded to throw the combat medals they had won at the police.

"Poopie," Andi asked, "are you gonna throw the medals you got in 'Nam?"

"Andi," answered Poopie, "the only thing I got in Vietnam was the clap."

Midfielder James "Poopie" Williams dodging against East Carolina.

○

Poopie was having trouble sleeping in his own apartment since there was always a lot of noise and arguing in the apartment next-door. It kept him up at night and was affecting his schoolwork and lacrosse play.

○

Bacon, Wayne, and Dickie Hall were all injured, and there was neither medical help nor full-time trainers on campus. I put in a call to the Johns Hopkins Athletic Center and spoke to Mr. Brandywine, the school's trainer for 30 years. "Brandy" allowed the guys to come over, and he took care of them. At first, the guys were leery of Brandy because he put them together in a whirlpool and threw in several bags of ice. It was freezing.

"Is this your nigger treatment?" asked Bacon sarcastically.

"No," laughed Brandy, "it's for everybody. Come here, watch." And he went over to a long table where a three-time All-American for Hopkins slept, and poured ice all over him.

The *Three Bears* smiled as they looked enviously around the athletic training facility. Ice was now the prescribed treatment for many sports injuries. The room was loaded with numerous modern whirlpools and long tables with players receiving all sorts of treatment from individual certified trainers.

Dickie, Wayne, and John joked about Morgan's training room, run by part-time trainer Butterfly, with its one antiquated whirlpool and two sets of unmatched barbells. And no ankle taping unless Butterfly felt you needed it. They rehashed the previous home game when Bacon and Wayne sandwich-checked an opponent and broke his leg. I was running around calling for Butterfly and medical assistance when Andi deadpanned, "What's Butterfly going to do, burn some incense?"

Butterfly often burned incense in the training room to hold down the stench from the adjoining men's room.

That was also the last game we played without an ambulance available. The injured player had to ride in a Morgan State tow truck to Union Memorial Hospital. I told Coach Banks that the USILA was going to kick us out if we didn't have an ambulance at all home games.

○

George Kelly coming up with a face-off against Lafayette.

An outstanding Morgan football player was very upset with his girlfriend when he found out she was screwing two or three other players on the team. What upset him more than anything was that she "made it" with Danny Bell, who had told everyone about it.

To try and make up for her indiscretions, the girlfriend had bought him a beautiful pair of brown leather platform shoes that cost the ungodly sum of $200. After finding out more about her infidelity, the football player grew incensed. He threw the new shoes into the urinal and pissed all over them.

"Screw that bitch," he screamed. Then he invited all of his other football teammates to piss on the platform shoes laying in the urinal. After about three weeks, almost everyone using the football bathroom in the field house had pissed on the shoes.

On a road trip for a scrimmage across town, Oliver Chambers walked onto the bus wearing a pair of brown leather platform shoes. The bus cleared out.

"What's wrong with you guys?" Oliver pleaded. "Bacon sold me these shoes for $35. They retail for $200. I know they're a little stained, but he said it was from the sun in the store window. That's why I got a discount!"

○

At one point I considered cutting Oliver Chambers from the team. He had missed a lot of practices, made costly mistakes on the field, and was constantly getting into trouble on the academic side of the school. Coaches Banks and Hurt could not stand him. Andi pleaded on Oliver's behalf. His major argument to me was "Please don't cut him. He's the only guy on the team with a smaller dick than me."

○

As time went by, the players began to decorate their sticks. Besides personalizing them, they emblazoned the sticks with green, black, and red paint—the colors of black nationalism—and jive sayings of the time; they also tied the gut and leather strings into dreadlocks.

After taking a philosophy course, Holley wrote on his stick, "I think, therefore I am," a quote from Descartes.

Freshman Dink saw it and asked, "What's that mean?"

Standing beside Poopie, Holley responded, "I'm a human being because I think. And that creates me. It's not wealth or a car, it's that we think. That's why we exist."

Poopie nodded, "I can dig it."

Dink reflected for a moment, rolled his trademark toothpick around his mouth and said, "That don't make sense." Then he walked away.

Poopie leaned over to Holley and remarked, "He don't *think*, therefore he *ain't*!"

"I can certainly dig that," responded Holley.

○

Wayne decided to move in with Nikki. They were both ready to get apartments and mutually agreed to get a place together. They didn't know if they were in love or what. They just knew that they were "tight" and trusted and respected one another.

The NFL draft was weighing heavily on Wayne's mind. Being drafted or signed as a free agent could mean a nice sized bonus. But he made a big mistake.

Coach Banks told his players that when the NFL scouts came around not to let them time anyone in a 40-yard dash. "Don't run unless I'm there" was what he said. Wayne forgot about it and it proved costly.

We were having a very long lacrosse practice when an NFL scout came down to the field and asked Wayne if he would run for him. The scout told him that the football coaches had sent him down to get a time. Wayne was very tired and shouldn't have run. Still wearing his lacrosse outfit, he ran a 4.7-second forty. He could have run a 4.4 or a 4.3 if he'd been fresh, and it kept him from being drafted by an NFL team.

○

With the team playing so well, it appeared the Bears could get to the NCAA Division II Tournament. If the team were selected, it meant every player would have to meet academic eligibility. Bacon was concerned. His grades were bad.

Bacon visited Poopie at his apartment. "I've decided what to call myself. John Jablai."

"I can dig it," said Poopie, "but what's it mean?"

"Well," said Bacon, "it means a 'rock' in Arabic."

"Listen," said Poopie, "you're missing the point. You need to change your name to someone on campus who has a common Muslim, African, or Arabic name and also has good grades. This will make you academically eligible. Ya know, like Cassius Clay changed his name to Muhammad Ali. Today, there are a lot of guys here at Morgan with that name. But understand me, John. You've got to have a name that is used by two or three students who are eligible. It's got to be a more common name, not just some pretty name you dream up for yourself. Okay?"

○

Morgan became overconfident. Towson State University wanted to postpone their home game because of a muddy field. I became unusually cocky and refused to let them cancel it.

The Towson officials moved the game from the rain-soaked stadium to their practice field. By game time, the weather had become cold and windy, and the practice field not only dried, but also was like playing in a dust bowl.

Unhappy with John Bacon's attitude and unmotivated play in practice, I decided not to start him against Towson. Unbeknownst to me, Andi had given Bacon Dexedrine tablets to use, one at a time, in the next two games. Bacon used both of them for the Towson game. By not playing, Bacon was "wired" to the max. He badly wanted to get into the game and run off the pills' false energy. Every 30 seconds, he nagged me to let him into the game. He also started running sprints behind the bench. I finally relented and put him in the game, but Bacon was so hyper that he overplayed the attackman he was guarding and fouled everyone, arguing with the refs after each penalty.

To make matters worse, the team kept thinking the Towson players and several fans in the bleachers were calling them "darkies." I took a timeout and demanded an apology from Towson's coach.

"Chipper," explained Carl Runk, Towson's coach, "our midfielder is named Jim Darcangelo and 'Darkie' is his nickname. The teammates and fans are just referring to him."

It got everybody laughing, and I felt like a schmuck.

The year before, the Bears had fallen behind highly ranked Towson State 8 to 0 before regrouping and barely losing 11 to 7. I felt, with a much stronger team, that this was the opportunity to defeat probably the best team in Division II lacrosse. Big mistake. Towson destroyed us 20 to 2 in the team's worst-ever defeat. Raymond and Wayne, the Bears' top scorers, were shut out, but Towson's star attackman, Bob Griebe, managed five goals and six assists against Andi.

○

Dave Raymond and Millie were strolling on the campus by the Murphy Fine Arts Center.

"Why'd you get an apartment, Dave?" she asked.

"Couldn't study in the dorms. Too noisy," answered Dave.

"I've seen some girls coming out of your place," said Millie.

"Tutors," replied Dave.

○

Scott, Dink, and Jacques were leaning on the ledge of the Student Union building aggravating Cherry, who had a girlfriend with him. Dumb move.

"What was the score?" asked Cherry.

"We beat 7-4," said Scott.

"Who beat?" asked Cherry.

"What do you mean, 'who beat'? You sound like an idiot!" said Scott.

The three started imitating the way Cherry talked, and Stanley got pissed. They were embarrassing him in front of his woman. Cherry chased them. Just as he grabbed Scott, he fell, scratching up his knee and tearing his pants.

Regaining his composure, Cherry said, "Tell Dink to come over here now," as he twisted Scott's arm back and up.

"Come on over, Dink," begged Scott.

"No damn way!" yelled Dink as he backed up. "You can break his arm off, Cherry, 'cause I ain't comin'!"

Just then, Stanley's girlfriend came over and began brushing the dirt off his clothes. It distracted him long enough for Scott to break away.

Attackman Dave Raymond (#28) shooting over East Carolina defensemen.

As a result, Scott and the freshmen hid for a few days. They ducked Stanley often after the incident.

○

Cherry had made the Kodak All-American Football Team. Everyone in the Baltimore area felt he definitely would be drafted in the early rounds by a National Football League team. When this didn't happen and Stanley signed with the New England Patriots as a free agent, he was dejected. But while I found it incomprehensible that Stanley hadn't been drafted, he seemed resigned to the inevitability of the fact.

I approached him and asked, "I don't understand, Stanley. How could you *not* be drafted? You're one of the best linebackers coming out of college."

Linebacker Stanley Cherry — Kodak All-American Football Team.

"I didn't eat enough cheese," Cherry responded.

"What do you mean you didn't eat enough cheese?" I asked. "You mean, like, to bulk up? I don't know if cheese is what you would want to eat a lot of . . . It's constipating . . ."

"No," interrupted Stanley. "Not actually eating cheese. 'Eating cheese' is the same as kissing ass. Okay? Because I didn't kiss the coaches' asses enough, they didn't push for me. Actually, they told the NFL scouts that I had a bad back and a bad attitude. Two things that just killed me."

O

After graduating from Morgan, Val Emery began teaching at City College, his alma mater. He became the first black lacrosse coach in the Baltimore Public School system when he was named head lacrosse coach of the junior varsity team. Val was also playing club lacrosse for the Towson Lacrosse Club and was hopeful that several of his former Morgan teammates would be joining him. If Wayne Jackson and Stan Cherry did not make it in professional football, Val hoped they too would play club lacrosse, and they could all continue to compete at this new level.

Since there was no professional lacrosse league in the '70s, most of the men who had played lacrosse at the collegiate level gravitated to club teams. The East Coast was where most club lacrosse was played, and the governing body was the United States Club Lacrosse Association. Players joined club teams so that they could relive their glory days on the weekends, motivated by the camaraderie and their great love of the game.

Club teams usually had two practice sessions on weekday evenings, and the games were played on weekends. Although the crowds seldom exceeded a thousand, the fans were usually die-hard lacrosse enthusiasts. Interestingly, while most of the players had been middle- and upper-class whites, those demographics were slowly shifting as Morgan's lacrosse program began funneling black players into the club leagues.

Club leagues presented great social and networking opportunities to their members. I encouraged my players to join these clubs after their college eligibility, assuring them that lacrosse would open many doors. Many club players were investment bankers, lawyers, insurance salesmen, and teachers, and they had great connections. This avenue to continue play (and the added benefits) was welcome to the Morgan postgraduates, or others whose college eligibility was up.

Club lacrosse, however, was not cheap. Players had to pay for their equipment and other related expenses. With the way sticks broke, expenses could easily run up to a few hundred dollars a year.

○

Morgan needed to win their last two games in order to make the NCAA tournament. Unfortunately, we lost the first of those games at Mount St. Mary's. The game, played in Emmitsburg in Western Maryland, drew a huge crowd to see the greatly improved Mount team enjoying another win in an outstanding season. Also, memories of the fight at Morgan in 1970 created a tense atmosphere.

At one point, play got out of control. One of the Mount's attackmen and Bacon had an altercation, and both were ejected from the game. Larry Levitt, an old friend and a former lacrosse great, was refereeing the game. After Bacon's ejection, I ran onto the field and talked to Larry. Miraculously, Bacon was allowed back into the game.

Amazed, Bacon asked me, "What did you say? What was it? What got me back in the game?"

I whispered back, "It's a Jewish thing."

One of those rare incestuous pluses for the Bears was Larry's relationship with Morgan lacrosse personnel. Levitt, Schnoo Snyder, and me were old friends and Zeta Beta Tau (ZBT) fraternity brothers from the University of Maryland. Schnoo played on the 1959 City team with Larry. And Bubbie and Danny Bell lived near Levitt's parents' grocery store. Levitt had known them since they were toddlers.

Of course, similar relationships among lacrosse officials and opposing teams' coaching staffs were a hundred times more pervasive, given their longer histories in the game.

When the team boarded the bus to leave Mount St. Mary's, almost everyone was in a somber mood. However, Scott, Dink, and Jacques, displaying their freshman immaturity, boarded the bus laughing and carrying on. Bacon lost it. He grabbed Scott and started choking him. Wayne pulled him off right before Scott blacked out.

○

Tyrone Scott graduated from Forest Park High School. He was an outstanding athlete who had played three years of varsity football and lacrosse. On the football team, Tyrone played wide receiver and defensive back. The team won two "B" Conference Championships.

Tyrone's early sports ambition was to run track. But, while he was out practicing with the track team during the spring of his sophomore year, the Forest Park lacrosse coach, Chuck Waesche, strolled over and asked, "Do you want to play a real game?" This was similar to how Waesche had recruited Miles Harrison Jr. a few years earlier.

Tyrone took one look at the lacrosse team practice and said, "I don't think so. Somebody could hit me on the head and kill me."

Coach Waesche gave him a stick and a ball, anyway, and let him take it home. Tyrone practiced for a few days, enjoying the stickwork, and decided he would try out for lacrosse. He loved the action, and his athletic ability got him on the varsity immediately. He played mostly midfield and some attack. Through playing lacrosse, Tyrone met Dink Brown from Edmondson and Jerna Jacques from Northwestern.

Tyrone enjoyed the trips to play the private schools: Gilman, Park School, John Carroll, and Cardinal Gibbons. He saw young kids walking around with sticks and told his teammates, "We're gonna get killed. These people have been playing all their lives."

While Forest Park had a fair lacrosse team, they had some upsets along the way. They outran the preppies and had a lot more heart than other teams. Tyrone's best game came against City one year when he scored four goals in a game. Forest Park won 5 to 4. Guarding him that day was Danny Bell.

Tyrone was a "B" student, and he made All-MSA in lacrosse.

He came from a family of 13 children, and he felt it was more important for him to get a job than pursue a college education. So he went to work for the London Fog Company making raincoats. He enjoyed it. He had money in his pocket, was helping out his mom, and was looking to buy a new car. Then, one afternoon, his mother and several sisters sat him down at the kitchen table and told him that somebody in the family had to give college a try.

Tyrone decided to attend Morgan where he thought he would play football. But he was a wide receiver, and Morgan was a running football team, rarely passing the ball.

So his sports passion turned to lacrosse. He knew he would play more lacrosse than football (where he probably wouldn't see much action). And he didn't want to be a second-stringer.

Tyrone hitchhiked to school every day, the money for his car having gone toward tuition. As a freshman at Morgan, Tyrone resumed his acquaintanceships from high school competition with Dink and Jacques. They were inseparable friends who became known as the "Gruesome Threesome."

○

A whirlwind season left Morgan with its final scheduled game, a must-win if we were to reach the playoffs. The opponent was Loyola, a team dead set on keeping the Bears out of the tournament. A win against the Bears would make the season for Loyola, but it was not to be. I asked the guys to "pour it on," knowing that only a big win would ensure one of the top spots in the Division II Tourney. Wayne Jackson and Dave Raymond scored ten goals between them in phenomenal performances. Morgan defeated Loyola 19 to 3.

It was unusual for me to tell the guys to go for an exaggerated win. I felt it was unsportsmanlike to beat a team by as many goals as possible. It was embarrassing, and I would not want to be in the reverse position. But, that time, I had no choice.

Morgan was selected to the National Collegiate Athletic Association Lacrosse Tournament for Division II teams and paired against perennial contender Washington College. A great team with a fabled tradition in lacrosse, they were located on the other side of the Chesapeake Bay Bridge in the small hamlet of Chestertown.

○

Now that we were gearing up for the Division II Tourney, it was more important than ever for the team to buckle down and get serious. So it bothered me that two key players seemed to be slacking off.

I confronted midfielder Leonard Spicer, asking why he hadn't played hard for the past couple games or in practice.

"It's my neck, Coach," explained Spicer. "I have trouble moving it, and anytime there's contact, it kills me."

"C'mon, Lenny," I urged. "You gotta suck it up. Be tough. Don't wimp out on me. Tell ya what. Go see Doctor Becker after practice and maybe he'll help you out. You probably just slept wrong."

"Anybody seen George Kelly?" I screamed to the team as I

turned away from Spicer. "Our face-off midfielder, and he's missed practice for three days."

"He's got makeup tests all week," said Nesbit. "He might even miss the game 'cause he's got a final exam Saturday."

Tyrone Scott whispered to Dink, "See, that's why ya can't go to class. You get caught up in all that academic crap."

○

Before going to bed that night, I received a phone call from Doctor Becker.

"Spicer has a broken neck," said Becker, "and it's been like that for a month. How the hell did he play?"

"Not as well as he did earlier in the season," I said. "Can he play Saturday?"

"Are you crazy?" replied Becker. "He's lucky he's not paralyzed. He's gonna be messed up for months."

"Jesus Christ! I didn't know. He never said anything. Will he be all right?"

"Yeah," said Becker. "We'll fix him up."

○

I called Kelly at home and told him to call his professors and reschedule his exams. But George was adamant about finishing up this week.

"You're very stubborn, George," I said. "You're letting down the team, and me."

"Sorry, Chip. I studied and I'm ready. I can't make the game."

"You're very selfish, George," I said, "but, the hell with it! At least I know you'll be back in school next year. Good luck!"

○

George Kelly grew up in east Baltimore on Wolfe Street, and he followed most of his friends to the newly built Northern High School, one of the better public schools at the time. Because of the large number of students attending, school was initially taught in double shifts. Kelly met Courtenay and Nesbit during the early shift.

George excelled at football and lacrosse. He was an All-State midfielder and defenseman in lacrosse, and he played quarterback on the football team. He was named to the All-State team during his senior year and was also inducted into the Northern High School Athletic Hall of Fame.

In addition, George was an honor student, but, surprisingly, he was not offered any scholarships. So the only place his parents could afford to send him was local Morgan State.

○

In New York, H. Rap Brown was found guilty and sentenced to Attica State Prison for five to fifteen years.

○

The team was in a huddle at Washington College right before the game began. I was telling defenseman Maurice Ashe to stay on Tom George, a great attackman, for the entire game.

"No matter where he goes," I said, "and I don't care if he goes to the bathroom . . . anywhere he goes, you're on him the whole time. Never leave him. Just like the guy at Frostburg."

"Anywhere?" repeated Ashe.

"Yeah, anywhere!" I said emphatically.

The game began and Washington College scored early. A school tradition was to shoot off two cannons whenever anyone scored. As soon as the cannons went off, Poopie and Holley, Vietnam vets, dove for cover. I had to call a timeout to calm them down. Washington College refused to silence the cannons.

Holley and Hall played great. They did the dirty work: got ground balls, took hits, set screens and picks, and delivered crunching body-checks. They were unselfish and wanted only to win.

The game was very close going into the last quarter. Down by a goal, we were in an extra-man situation when Washington College deflected a pass. They retrieved the ball and sped downfield on a fast break. Their star midfielder, Bob Shriver, was racing toward Morgan's goal, alone. Courtenay kept yelling for Ashe to slide, in other words to leave his man and pick up Shriver coming in with the ball. Ashe looked at Courtenay, looked at the attackman he was guarding, and remembered that I said never to leave his man. So Ashe stayed with Tom George, and the fast-breaking midfielder came straight toward the goal. Shriver scored without anyone challenging him.

Afterwards, Courtenay screamed at Ashe, "Why didn't you slide?"

"Well," said Ashe, "Chip said to stay with George anywhere he went and I did."

Had Kelly and Spicer played, Morgan may have won, but I never used it as an excuse. I respected Kelly's choice, and anguished over Spicer's broken neck for years. We lost 11 to 7.

O

The team elected Poopie captain for the next season. At his apartment, the players discussed how the previous season had gone, and partied quite a bit.

After the guys left, there were loud noises coming from the apartment next-door. Poopie opened his door to look out. The dope dealer/pimp was smacking his girlfriend around. He stopped when he realized Poopie was glaring at him.

"You close that fuckin' door if you don't want a piece of me," the drug dealer yelled menacingly at Poopie.

O

Wayne played for the South team as Morgan's representative for the North/South All-Star Game at Princeton. Unlike Miles Harrison Jr., who had experienced racism and related problems, Wayne had a very positive experience.

On his first night, Wayne was just about to go to sleep when the other players barged into his room and encouraged him to join them. They had a few beers in the dorm and then went to a nightclub to party and dance.

Wayne did not want to drink too much because he wanted to be in top form during practices and the game. But he still had fun with all the other players who got blitzed. After the nightclub, they went skinny-dipping in a fountain right in the middle of Princeton's campus. When security came, they just told the guys to "be cool."

Wayne, who had never met his opponents as "real" people, finally got to talk to some of the guys he had played against. One reminded him about the Towson State/Morgan game where a fight had erupted and a lot of players converged to beat up Wayne. In defense, Wayne had swung his stick at anyone who charged him. Turns out that his stick had hit a Towson midfielder in the face, knocking out several teeth. Wayne never knew this, and although the Towson players were trying to pummel Morgan's guys, he said, "Please tell the guy that I'm sorry."

At the dinner the evening before the game, Wayne received his All-American certificate for the third year in a row.

During practice for the North/South Game, Wayne impressed the other All-Stars with his unique style of play, but somehow got the coach pissed off. Wayne felt that the lack of the coach's favor would affect his chances to see action during the game. But, it didn't matter since Wayne's South team so dominated the North that everybody got to play a lot. During the game, Wayne was coming in for a wide-open shot, but instead of shooting, he fed it off to another player. It was such a great feed that the player never even saw it coming and missed it. Wayne heard me in the stands yelling, "Shoot it!" As Wayne ran up field later in the game, I screamed out, "Just shoot the ball! Forget these other guys!"

SUMMER 1973

My wife wanted to go out on a Sunday afternoon, so I told her, "That's a great idea. Let's picnic."

I took her to a lacrosse summer league game where many of my Morgan team members were playing. I spread out a blanket and placed the picnic basket on it. The game was enjoyable, but it wasn't exactly what my wife had in mind.

○

Wayne called and told me that not only didn't the NFL draft him, but also that his chances to sign as a free agent were slim. Therefore, he had decided to play in the new World Football League.

But, after three weeks, Wayne could not take the "politics" of the league. He left his professional athletic career behind him, and returned home to Nikki.

○

Against the advice of prison officials, Ochiki Young decided to enroll in the University Without Walls program in order to complete Morgan State's degree requirements. New Morgan president, King V. Cheek, had created the program.

"What the hell do you want an education for?" asked one prison official. "You're gonna be here for the rest of your life."

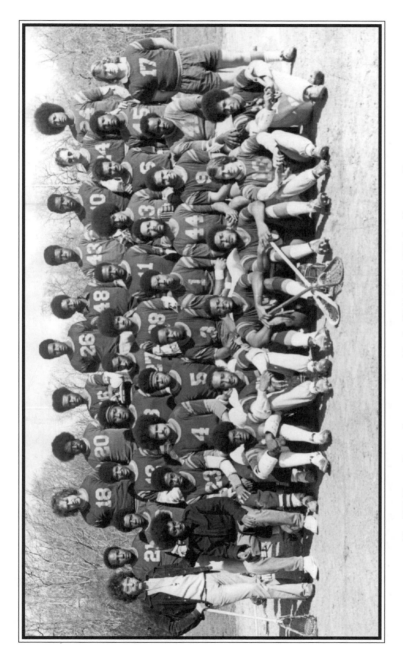

The 1973 Morgan Bears who were selected for the NCAA Division II National Lacrosse Tournament.

CHAPTER 8

REBOOTIN'

FALL 1973

I was feeling optimistic about our chances this year, even though we were suffering the loss of some of our best players. Before the year was out, we would lose a key member of our team under tragic circumstances.

The New England Patriots cut Stanley Cherry early. At the urging of Raymond Chester, a teammate from Morgan who was now playing for the Baltimore Colts, Cherry received a tryout from the Colts and made the team. He was elated, and became very devoted to Chester and Lydell Mitchell, two All-Pro players for the Colts who encouraged Stanley's signing with the general manager, Joe Thomas.

O

I was meeting with the players and advised them that the Intercollegiate Lacrosse Association had approved "Fall Ball," and that they'd be able to play four games. Among the teams we would compete against were the University of Maryland and the Naval Academy, two great programs with winning lacrosse traditions.

I explained to the players that we would practice two days a week prior to each game.

"Everybody's got to be to practice on time. It's very important."

I stressed the fact that I had a regular job and had to use my personal or compensatory leave time to be at practice. "Also," I added, "Schnoo Snyder won't be with us any longer. He's going to be an apprentice horse trainer and . . ." My remaining comments were drowned out by loud cheering.

○

I stood on the field at Hughes Stadium waiting for most of the team while watching the two white players. Andi was shooting at the goal, warming up Courtenay. Earlier, Courtenay had again whined to me about wanting to play midfield this season.

"Next year," I promised, disingenuously.

The only other players there were my new recruits who were mostly from out of state.

The younger local players: Scott, Dink, Jacques, and entering freshmen, had public school backgrounds. They came to Morgan in '72 and '73 without the strong competition that Wayne, Cherry, Hall, and Holley had faced. This was due to the separation of the private and public school leagues. As a result, the level of play in the public schools diminished dramatically.

Due to the general decline of Baltimore City public school lacrosse, I looked to the north for recruits in Long Island, New York and New Jersey to supplement Morgan's local contingent.

Dink, Scott, and Jacques were playing lacrosse catch in Mondawmin Shopping Center, one of the local malls. Instead of balls, they were throwing empty liquor miniatures across the aisles, over the shelves, and anywhere else they could. Finally, they were chased out of the mall by security.

As they rode to practice in Scott's girlfriend's car, they dressed and laughed about me and CPT (colored people's time).

"Poor, dumb Chip," said Scott. "He truly believes that if you tell niggers a specific time, we'll show up late; so he tells us an earlier time and figures we'll be there when he *really* needs us."

"Yeah," added Dink, "like when he told us the bus was leaving for the playoffs at Washington College at ten a.m. and it wasn't due till noon."

Jacques, who was taping his high socks to his legs, joined in, "So those fools, Courtenay and Andi, show up at ten and have to wait like saps till Chip shows at eleven-thirty; and we post at twelve!"

"That's why we gotta punish Chip when he tells us to be on the field by one o'clock and really intends practice to start at three p.m.," said Scott.

"Well, it's a quarter till four and Chip's losing his compensatory time from work," said Dink, "so we better hurry."

○

Very satisfied with Dave Raymond's progress, I recruited another Long Island, New York attack prospect—John Workman—from Uniondale High. He was a thin, quick athlete with ambidextrous stickwork. Unlike Bacon and Raymond, Workman was extremely shy and quiet.

I was also very pleased with the potential I saw in two local products. One pleasant surprise was William "Buck" Turnage from Northwestern, the brother of Tyrone Scott's girlfriend, "Boots." The other was Tyrone "Puddie" Jones from Edmondson High, who came with All-State credentials.

Puddie grew up in Edmondson Village and attended Thomas Jefferson Elementary School. One day he saw some white boys playing lacrosse. He watched for a while and asked if he could hold a stick. One of the boys actually gave Puddie an extra one he had.

Puddie entered Edmondson in 1970 and played varsity lacrosse for three years. He made the All-MSA Team and was First Team "B" Conference. He ran on the same midfield as Dink Brown, who lived around the corner.

Dink liked money a lot and had a paper route, working every season except the spring. He played varsity lacrosse in the eleventh and twelfth grades.

Edmondson High's program in lacrosse and other sports was on a downward trend as a result of the building of two new schools in west Baltimore: Southwestern High and Walbrook High. Many players who would normally have gone to school at Edmondson went to these new Baltimore City public schools.

Puddie came to Morgan in the fall of 1973. The summer before, Puddie had met Scott and Jacques through his friend, Dink. They were throwing the ball around in Dink's backyard when Scott said, "You'll be my ground-ball man," meaning that Puddie would help retrieve the ball for Scott and be his "gofer."

Puddie took an immediate dislike to Scott. As an "All-World" player (in his mind) at Edmondson, Puddie replied, "I don't do just that—I do it all!"

Puddie was very excited to attend Morgan. He was a very naive, strong, silent type. His first day on campus, he went to the student bookstore and bought a hat, a bag, and a shirt, all inscribed with "Morgan State." Bubbie, Oliver Chambers, and Scott saw Puddie, and they got on him so hard over buying all the Morgan paraphernalia that Puddie was humiliated.

"How much did you pay for that?" asked Oliver Chambers. "We could have stolen that for half the price." The guys started calling Puddie "Mr. Morgan, Mr. Morgan." After that, Puddie never wore or carried any of the Morgan paraphernalia again.

Early in his college career, Puddie went home often, ignoring many of the numerous parties thrown on campus. That was until he began hanging out with the Gruesome Threesome. Dink, Scott, and Jacques introduced Puddie to girls and trouble.

Scott always knew where the parties and the women were. Anytime any of the guys were bored, they just followed Scott, Jacques, and Dink to the action.

○

On the hallowed grounds of the Naval Academy in Annapolis, Maryland, the Ten Bears played very well, especially Poopie, who controlled most of the face-offs. We lost 4 to 3 but weren't embarrassed. Bullock played his best game, "wasting" the attackman he was guarding and taunting him by calling him "swabby." Andi, aware of Navy's great lacrosse tradition, played scared, but the rest of the Bears were not afraid.

At one point in the last quarter, with the score tied at three, Andi asked a Navy midfielder, "Are you sure you guys are the varsity?"

As the Navy scrimmage ended, a black woman in her seventies approached me. She introduced herself as Mrs. Smithers and informed me that, though now retired, she had worked at the Naval Academy, in the kitchen, for almost 40 years.

"I would appreciate the opportunity," she said, "to speak to your players, to tell them how proud I am of their efforts, and to tell them a story."

I reluctantly agreed. Since this was a Fall Ball scrimmage and the players had come in their own cars, they were anxious to leave Annapolis and return to Morgan. I wasn't sure they'd be willing to hang around too much longer.

I grabbed Poopie, whom I knew exerted influence on the players, and asked him to get the guys together for just a brief moment. Poopie quickly corralled the players. Mrs. Smithers came over, congratulated the team, and began to tell her story.

"Although I am very proud to have worked at the Naval Academy for many decades, seeing you young black men play so well against Navy has given me a different type of pride, and I want to tell you why. I'll be quick because I know your attention spans aren't what they should be at your age.

"You see, back when World War II started, Harvard University brought their lacrosse team to Annapolis to play against the Naval Academy. It was 1941 and Harvard had one of the first Negro players, a young man named Lucien Alexis. Navy refused to play the game because they wouldn't compete against a black man. The Academy officials told Harvard's coach that if he benched Alexis, Navy would bench a player of comparable worth. If the coach refused, Navy would forfeit the game. At the same time, the Superintendent of the Naval Academy was phoning Harvard officials to demand that Alexis be benched.

"Well, it was pretty tense on the field. I just watched as the Harvard athletic director initially refused their demands and said that Navy could forfeit the game. He was not going to bench his black player. But, finally, after a couple of long distance phone calls, the Harvard people gave in. The athletic director instructed the lacrosse coach to bench Mr. Alexis.

"I felt so bad for that young man," she continued. "He returned home right away, very despondent. This incident did not, however, go unnoticed. There were a lot of protests from the students at Harvard and other outside groups who heard about what had happened. Howls of indignation came from the American Federation of Labor and the NAACP, which felt that this was hypocrisy, especially during the war. They were very upset."

"Who won the game?" screamed out Dink.

"Well, it wasn't Harvard," responded Mrs. Smithers. "Navy must have won something like ten or twelve to nothing. But that isn't what anyone remembered. Of course, times have changed and the Naval Academy has come a long way. They finally admitted a black in 1945, and many fine, young black men have played all sports, including lacrosse, for Navy over the years.

"But I've been waiting . . . I've been waiting for you young men to come for a long time; and I'm just so proud of you."

The players who had been so anxious to get to their cars and drive home now stood around. One by one they shook Mrs.

Smithers' hand and gave her a hug. And then Scott said, "I wish you would have told us this story earlier, because then we'd have really kicked Navy's butt!"

○

The Navy game concluded the fall season. The upcoming spring schedule was going to be particularly challenging. Wayne, Cherry, and Dickie Hall had all completed their eligibility, and every opponent would be gunning for Morgan.

○

The night after the Navy game Poopie awoke to another altercation next-door. Still charged up over the game, he dressed quickly and stormed out of his apartment. Barging into a half-open door, he found himself in the middle of a drug deal gone awry. Poopie was shot twice and also stabbed.

I got a phone call at three a.m. from John Bacon who told me that Poopie had been killed.

○

At the funeral, there was very little said. Everyone was too choked up to talk. A large and eclectic mix of mourners attended the funeral. Poopie came from a family of lawyers and educators, and he had numerous friends from his four years in the service and his years at Morgan. His popularity spread among people from all social classes. Some of the players and I were pallbearers. The team dedicated the coming '74 season to him.

Poopie's brother, Charlie Williams, a prominent attorney, was there. He knew how much lacrosse had meant to Poopie, and he told me that he would buy new uniforms for the team. (They were still wearing old football jerseys.) "We'll have a black armband on the left sleeve with Poopie's number, 25, on the uniform," I promised.

Meanwhile, an altercation was taking place by Poopie's grave. It was rumored that there was an African-American superstition that the last woman at the grave was the deceased's true love. Since Poopie had a few girlfriends, a minor fistfight had broken out among several contenders, each wanting to be the last to pay her respects by Poopie's burial plot.

○

Schnoo Snyder showed up unexpectedly at Poopie's funeral. He was now living in northern Virginia, minutes from Washington, D.C., doing a sports talk show on local radio.

"I came to pay my respects. I liked Poopie. He was dedicated. Plus, he attended City College," he explained.

"That's commendable, Schnoo," I said, "but Poopie considered you an asshole for always knocking the players."

Schnoo laughed. He had a conspiratorial look on his face as he pulled me aside.

"I've been thinking about how good you said Dunbar High's basketball team is, and your ludicrous supposition that they can beat DeMatha, number one in Washington and number one in the U.S. We could make a lot of money pairing these two up."

I knew what a manipulator Snyder was and asked, "What do you mean 'we.' Where do I fit in?"

"Chippy," said Snyder, "you have credibility. I can get DeMatha 'cause I know their coach, but the Baltimore City schools won't fall for my pitch. But they love your ass!"

Reluctantly, I agreed to promote the game with Snyder. DeMatha High and the city public schools would receive cash guarantees, and Schnoo and I would split the rest of the profits (after paying the Baltimore Civic Center its fees).

The game was a natural. Each team had over three-year unbeaten streaks. DeMatha, led by Adrian Dantley, was considered the best high school team in the country. Dunbar, coached by the legendary Sugar Cain, had a prolific scoring guard named Skip Wise, a player who many considered the best prospect to ever grow up in Baltimore.

The deals were struck. Tickets were priced at four dollars each, and it looked as if, based on presales and the media promotions, Schnoo and I would have around $30,000 to split.

○

Tiger Davis and Oliver Chambers were in a crowd of onlookers outside of the heavily guarded Howard County Courthouse in Ellicott City awaiting the outcome of the five-year-delayed Rap Brown case.

The trial ended quickly after Judge MacGill accepted the recommendation of State's Attorney Kinlein. In a plea bargain session with Brown's attorney, Edward C. Broege, the State dropped arson and incitement to riot charges in exchange for a misdemeanor charge of failure to appear for trial three years earlier.

Before passing sentence, Judge MacGill asked Brown several standard questions to establish competency.

"How much education have you had?" asked MacGill.

"Not much," answered Rap facetiously. "Three years of college."

Brown was sentenced to a year in jail to run concurrently with the New York sentence. Also, the unlawful flight charge by the FBI was dropped.

Rap Brown was now a follower of Islam, having converted while awaiting trial on Rikers Island.

Outside, Oliver approached Tiger.

"I guess after Rap becomes a Muslim, he'll change his name. Right?"

"That's correct," answered Tiger.

"Where'd he get the name 'Rap'?" asked Oliver.

"Growing up in Baton Rouge he was quite the wordsmith," said Tiger. "He could create and rhyme in a heartbeat. Then he'd recite his 'raps' in a game called 'Dozens' where guys would try to knock each other through this form of poetry. It could get *very* cruel."

(Hubert Geroid Brown, a.k.a. H. Rap Brown, and his friends growing up in Louisiana in the '50s and '60s were "rapping" over 20 years before it became a music phenomenon.)

WINTER 1973-74

At the annual USILA Lacrosse Convention, Washington and Lee's Coach Emmer scheduled Morgan again. I explained that this was going to be a rebuilding year, but Emmer tended not to believe me after last spring's close game.

As usual, the William and Mary coach ducked me.

○

Vowing not to have a repeat of 1972, I was adamant about the team being ready despite the losses of Wayne Jackson, Poopie, and several other outstanding players. Since the team was potentially weaker than last year, practices began earlier, and in the snow.

During the first two practices, Tyrone Scott was dogging it, not hustling at all. It was upsetting some of the players, so I approached Tyrone with a deal.

"If you can beat me in a mile run around the track, you won't have to run in practice anymore."

I was wearing a suit, topcoat, and hard shoes, but was in decent shape, having run regularly over the years. I considered myself somewhat fast at distance running, and didn't believe that Tyrone could beat me.

Tyrone hung slightly behind me for the first three laps. I was running as fast as I could. Suddenly, Scott began taunting and running circles around me. My breathing became labored. Then Tyrone sprinted to the finish, beating me by over a hundred yards.

Everyone was laughing. Other team members challenged me to a similar race.

"I lied," I announced breathlessly to Tyrone. "What I meant to say was 'If you don't run in practice, you can't make the trip and play at Washington and Lee.' Ha, ha, ha."

○

Sheldon Freed was an All-American defenseman at the University of Baltimore, and a stellar club lacrosse player. I brought him on early in the spring to coach the defense two days a week. I had recruited a junior college All-American defenseman, Mendoza Wallace, from Farmingdale, New York to help form a good nucleus for Freed to coach. Plus, Sheldon was able to switch George Kelly to defense and work with Aaron Glover and several others to refine their game and learn the art of defense. Sheldon was considering applying to dental school at the time.

I needed all of the assistance I could garner on defense since it was the Bears' weakest area. Also, unlike Snyder, I could really count on Freed.

Schnoo Snyder was dropping by practices again, but his focus had changed. He no longer berated or tried to coach the players. Instead, he walked around with me during drills and scrimmages going over the plans for the mythical high school basketball championship of the United States—Dunbar vs. DeMatha.

"Ya know, Schnoo," I said, "I'm gonna be away for the game, taking the family to Miami for four days."

"Don't worry about a thing," assured Schnoo. "I'll take care of it all on 'game day.' I just need you to get a bunch of the lacrosse players to work security for me; cover the gates around the Civic Center where people could possibly sneak in. I'll pay each of 'em ten bucks."

I called the players together and asked for volunteer security guards.

"Ten bucks!" exclaimed George Kelly. "That's worse than slave labor."

"But George," said Snyder, "you'll get to see the game for free. And I'll treat everyone to lunch."

Twelve guys volunteered, and Snyder was elated.

○

George Kelly was always tormenting Millie about how he saw Dave with one girl or another to make her jealous. Sometimes Kelly would even take Millie to a party where he knew Dave would be. Then he would point and say, "Look, there's Dave dancing over there with that pretty girl. What's going on, Millie?"

Scott, Dink, and Jacques also gave Millie grief. At Morgan basketball games, she would be doing cheers and difficult gymnastic moves, which would sometimes end with an impressive standing split where she lifted her leg and held it up near her head. At that point, the guys would stand up and applaud Dave. "Hey," they'd scream, "that's 'cause of you, Dave. That's why she can do that."

○

Millie basically lived in Hurt Gymnasium cheering on the teams—basketball, wrestling, and swimming. She also spent a lot of time typing Dave's term papers. She was a topnotch student during her first two years of college. After that, Millie went through a major philosophical adjustment, which had a dramatic effect on her grades. They dropped.

She became a revolutionary. Millie's Social Science teacher taught her about Vietnam, civil rights, protests, and, most of all, the separatism on the Morgan campus—the two-class system that dealt as much with the "haves" and the "have-nots" as the different skin shades of black. This class and teacher enlightened her.

Millie found injustice in the fact that Morgan had not been given university status when other similarly ranked, but predominantly white, colleges in the Baltimore metropolitan area had achieved this status.

Millie became outspoken over the subculture of separatism at Morgan State College. She began wearing army fatigues. In contrast, Millie's roommate was a "black American princess" who had a different tam for each outfit (at least 50). Millie's parents did not approve of her revolutionary ideas, and were afraid it would distract her from her studies. Dave was proud of her.

SPRING 1974

In the locker room after practice, some players, emulating Cherry and the other graduates, were dragging some freshmen into the showers by their taped-up socks threatening to rape them. Andi and Courtenay were staring at Ashe, who was very well endowed. Scott yelled to Ashe, "You're not putting that cock to any good use. You ought to loan it to me."

O

Afterwards, the guys walked up into the gym where a Japanese karate expert was conducting an exhibition. He was throwing all kinds of volunteers around, challenging everyone. And then Cherry strolled in, volunteered, and destroyed the "expert."

The noise from the karate match was deafening, causing Athletic Director Banks to come down from his office to reprimand the players because of the noise and their foul mouths. Meanwhile, I was over with the basketball team, close to convincing Marvin Webster, the "Human Eraser," to practice with the lacrosse team. Basketball Coach Frazier saw us and went ballistic. In actuality, Coack Frazier and I were friends, but when he saw me with Webster, he knew my motive.

O

There were times when the lacrosse team had to wait to practice on the Hughes Stadium field. Sometimes ROTC used it for parade formations. The lacrosse players would wait impatiently at the top of the stadium.

Players like Bullock occupied their time by winging lacrosse balls down on the field, breaking up the formations.

The ROTC cadets would break rank upon seeing the lobbed hard rubber balls coming towards them, screaming out, "Incoming!"

○

Danny Bell had a brutal fall academic semester, and appeared to be ineligible for lacrosse in the spring. "Hipped" to using an African or Muslim name, he searched about campus for an achieving student whose name he could use when I turned in the team's roster to the Registrar's Office.

Suddenly, he noticed a commotion at the Administration Building. A large crowd had formed and was listening to an energetic speaker. Dave Raymond was standing on the periphery of the crowd and Bell sidled up to him.

"What's happening, Dave?" he asked.

"This dude's got a smooth rap. Trying to get the school a radio station."

The student activist was Kweisi Mfume, a.k.a. Frizzell Gray. A transfer student from the Community College of Baltimore, Mfume had turned his life around from his gangster past. He was a part-time D.J. from James Brown's black-owned WEBB radio station who mixed music with discussions of the black struggle, called "Ebony Reflections." He had developed a popular following.

Morgan State had been stalled by state bureaucrats from establishing a campus radio station in their bid for an FCC license. Since it wasn't a priority to the college's administration, nothing was moving forward, and the students were angry.

"How ya spell Kweisi's name?" asked Bell, getting out a pen and paper.

"I don't know," answered Dave. "Why?"

"He's a smart talker. I'll bet he's got at least a "B" average," said Bell. "Sound it out for me and I'll figure it out later."

"Kwah-ee-see Oom-foo-may," said Raymond. "But he's too well known. Chip would catch on. He knew him from down on the Avenue."

"Come on," said Bell, "Chip ain't got a clue about what's happening around here!"

○

On the bus trip to Washington and Lee, the team stopped at a Howard Johnson's in the small southern Virginia town of Staunton. Some of the guys didn't pay their tab because the cashier refused to acknowledge their presence. She was either completely prejudiced or just scared of blacks. But because they left without paying, the state police were called. One trooper dramatically blocked the bus. Reluctantly, I resolved the problem by paying for all the meals.

At Washington and Lee that evening, I decided to impose a curfew. I didn't want any trouble—no hanging around the town of Lexington or playing midnight basketball.

"We really need to be focused for this game!"

At bed check, I was alarmed to find most of the guys missing. Upon further inspection, I found them in the bathroom watching porno films. One of the films had some scenes of men performing oral sex on women. Most of the black players were disgusted.

"Eeewww . . . You don't do that, do you, Coach?" asked Bullock.

"Yeah," I answered, now staring at the footage.

"Eeewww . . ." the guys yelled, "and Andi does it, too!"

The players were always tormenting Andi about oral sex with women. They would scream at him, "You ate that stanky pussy?" ("Stanky" was one of their favorite adjectives.) They also warned Andi of the potential correlation between having oral sex with a woman and a man. "If you lick the hole, you'll suck the pole."

O

Puddie thought he would have some time to develop as a position player, but after Poopie was killed, he had to be the face-off man and center midfielder. His experience in these positions began at Washington and Lee, his first college game. Deep down, Puddie felt he was not ready. It wasn't like the high school B Conference where he dominated. As a freshman, he figured there would be plenty of time to learn more and to develop his lacrosse game for university-level competition. But Poopie's death changed everything.

Puddie had to think much more than he had ever done before. It wasn't instinctive physical lacrosse. He had to quickly comprehend the various defensive and offensive schemes that changed so often at the collegiate level. There were so many different plays to learn: the one-three-two, the two-two-two, the one-four-one, and so on. Often, Puddie got lost on offense and defense because he was confused. There were pressures that he had never before experienced.

Also, Puddie had never played in front of big crowds. He came to recognize the loud roar at away games as the sound of losing.

Recruited to replace Wayne Jackson, Puddie didn't play up to his capabilities or past achievements, and he began to feel despondent.

During the Washington and Lee game, Puddie had his nose broken. Ted Bauer, a very skilled All-American midfielder, pushed his stick backwards on a face-off and it went through Puddie's facemask. Blood began spurting out, running down his shirt. The game was stopped and, within minutes, an ambulance appeared on the field. Paramedics had to reset Puddie's nose while he lay bleeding on the ground. They hurried him away to the emergency room of the Lexington, Virginia hospital.

Washington and Lee destroyed Morgan State 16 to 4. Our team was young, out-skilled, and had committed too many penalties. The one bright spot was defenseman Curt Anderson who had shut down W & L's top scorer, Sam Inglehardt. He did it by slipping the bottom of his stick down into the back of Inglehardt's pants and keeping it there most of the game.

That Saturday night, when the team returned to Morgan, Courtenay tried to start his car and it wouldn't turn over. He opened the hood and discovered that the battery was missing.

Courtenay went back to the field house and complained loudly about it to the other players. One of them, Virgil Love, who had a slow, deep, Southern accent, asked, "What kind of battery was it, Courtenay, a Diehard?"

"I dunno," answered Courtenay.

"Do you think it was a Diehard?" asked Virgil again.

"What does it matter what brand it was? It was stolen anyhow!" screamed a frustrated Courtenay.

○

Miles Harrison Jr. returned from school in Philadelphia and stopped by a practice to visit. I introduced Miles to the team, telling them that he had recently completed medical school and was now a doctor.

I asked Miles to check Bubbie's injured shoulder. When Miles walked over to examine him, Bubbie freaked out and moved away.

"I don't want no damn black doctor touching me," he yelled as Miles looked at me dejectedly.

Midfielder Morgan Holley preparing to dodge against Ohio Wesleyan.

○

After Poopie's death, the "sessions" shifted to Dave Raymond's apartment. However, they still listened to Poopie's *Santana* albums. Some guys drank beer and others got high, smoking a very potent strain of pot. Andi, who thought he was black even when he was straight, had an adverse reaction to the high-quality marijuana.

In a panic, he confided to Dave, "My nose is getting wider, my hair kinky, and now I feel my lips growing bigger. My God, I'm turning into Bullock!!"

"Andi, cool it," said Dave. "Your hair was always kinky."

○

Puddie missed the second game of the season because of his broken nose. Morgan lost a close one to Ohio Wesleyan 9 to 8. Puddie returned for the Villanova game, but after a few minutes out on the field, he was kneed in the side of the head and wobbled up dazed. He had a concussion. Dizzy and lightheaded, he forgot what team we were playing against and what the score was. Dink ran over and escorted him off the field. Again, he had to be sent to a hospital. Morgan did, however, beat Villanova 10 to 5.

After three games in the new uniforms bought by Poopie's brother, our players were happy to discover that their new outfits were confusing opponents. They would often call out, "I've got number 25" or "Pick up number 25," inadvertently referring to Poopie's old number emblazoned on the black armband.

○

After my vacation in Miami, I asked Andi Arenson how the DeMatha game had gone. I had heard that Dunbar won, ending DeMatha's winning streak at 47 games in a row, before a near-sellout crowd at the Civic Center. Adrian Dantley had been held in check by sophomore center, Larry Gibson, and Skip Wise scored 21 points in the last quarter to break the game wide open.

"Andi," I said, "I haven't been able to locate Snyder. How'd everything go?"

"It was crazy," he began. "We decided that we should make more than the ten dollars for the day. So, instead of keeping kids from sneaking in for free, we charged them two dollars apiece, half the admission price. Each of us cleared at least eighty dollars. But Snyder caught a couple of the guys and got real pissed off."

○

Puddie missed two more games because of his concussion, and then returned for the Loyola contest. For a freshman who hadn't played an entire game yet, he was playing very well. But in the middle of the second quarter, his hamstring pulled. This injury kept him out for an even longer period of time.

○

At Morgan's Student Center, a few of the Ten Bears were play-ing video games. Several female groupies were watching. One of the girls was known for going from player to player, becoming the girl-friend of a different one each week. But like clockwork, every other week, one of her ex-boyfriends came down with the clap. By April, half a dozen lacrosse players had the clap, but were too embarrassed to disclose it. A week later, I walked into the locker room while ten guys were "pissing and moaning." Confronting them about the clap, I made them immediately follow me out of the field house and over to the student health clinic where they were all given penicillin shots.

O

Danny Bell had missed most practices and games through half the season, so when he showed up early one afternoon to work out, I decided to have a chat with him.

"Danny," I said, "the African name you gave me last month is familiar. How did you come about choosing it?"

"It's a black thing, Chip," said Danny. "You wouldn't understand."

"Try me," I said as I grabbed a lacrosse stick and played catch with Bell. "By the way, what does Kweisi Mfume mean?"

"Well," said Danny as he stammered for an answer, "it means, uhm . . . ya see, it's a loose translation for . . . er . . . a . . . Prince of Darkness or Blackness."

"That's interesting," I said as I threw the ball purposely to Bell's left side where he normally had trouble catching it. "'Cause there's another guy with the same name on campus. I know him from years ago when I first worked on Pennsylvania Avenue. Anyhow, I ran into him the other day, and he said Kweisi Mfume meant 'Conquering Son of Kings.'"

"Yeah," said Danny, "that's still another looser translation."

O

In a game against UMBC, Courtenay called a time-out and ran over to me. "These stinking refs are racist! One of 'em called me a monkey!" he screamed.

"Calm down," I said. "Did he call the *team* 'monkeys' or just you?"

"Just me. Why?" asked Courtenay.

"What's the matter with you?" I said. "You're five-foot-three and you're *white*. So what if he called you a monkey! It's a term of endearment. Get back in the game."

UMBC beat Morgan for the fourth year in a row, 11 to 6, and Puddie, who was once again healthy, was thrown out of the game for fighting.

O

Bubbie had a calming effect on Pops the bus driver. On a trip to play Georgetown University in Washington D.C., Oliver Chambers stole a Mother's Day gift, salt and pepper shakers shaped like birds, from a Ho Jo's. Afterwards, Bubbie and Oliver argued the immorality of thieving for the rest of the trip. Pops sided with Bubbie.

○

Dave Raymond and Millie were partying at Scott's house with the guys. Courtenay and Andi were also there. Andi loved trying to act black, but it bothered Courtenay. The players relished in teasing Courtenay, but Millie stood up for him.

She always enjoyed his companionship and made up special cheers with the other cheerleaders for him. They became very friendly. Courtenay always looked to Millie for advice and interpretation. "What are the guys saying? What are they doing? What does that mean?" Courtenay was slow to understand the black culture.

○

I called and left countless messages for Schnoo Snyder following my return from Miami to check on my share of the Dunbar/DeMatha game, but to no avail. Finally, I saw him one evening at the Costas Inn, a crab house and restaurant in eastern Baltimore County.

"Schnoo," I asked, "where's my share of the game receipts? And where ya been?"

"I haven't called," answered Snyder, "'cause there's nothing to discuss; except that some of your players ripped me off. Other than that, we didn't make any profit."

I was livid, but wore a poker face; something Dean DeCosta had taught me to do in emotional situations involving business.

"Eleven thousand fans at four bucks apiece and there's no profit? Is that what you're saying?" I asked. "Or did my players rip you off for forty grand?"

Snyder continued eating his steamed crabs and spoke quickly.

"It's not easy to explain," he said, "but here goes. The City School Board and DeMatha demanded more of a percentage. And the Civic Center also upped the ante. Your players let a few hundred kids in for one or two bucks a head, costing me a couple thou'. So when it was all over, we only made four hundred dollars."

I was incredulous. Snyder stopped pounding on the steamed crabs and stood up. He wiped his hands and went into his pocket.

"Here's two hundred," he said. "We're even; but believe me, I lost more."

He was right. I discovered a few years later that Schnoo had lost about $35,000 of *our* money—at the racetrack.

○

I left practice early one day to take in the Perry Hall/Dulaney lacrosse game and evaluate senior attackman, Mike Walsch. I brought along George Kelly, whose opinion I valued. Perry Hall High School was located in eastern Baltimore County a few miles north of the city line beyond the Baltimore Beltway. My mother-in-law was the librarian at Perry Hall, and also served as a semi-scout for good lacrosse players I could entice with the Other-Race Grant.

Since I could only realistically recruit black players or marginally talented white players for Morgan State College, I had developed a keen eye for assessing raw ability and potential in high school lacrosse athletes. I could not compete for the Grade A players who were heavily recruited by colleges with more financial aid and lacrosse tradition.

I watched Mike Walsch as he dodged around the Dulaney defenseman and deftly passed the ball to a cutting midfielder whose shot bounced high off the chest of the goalie. Walsch, at 5'10" and 160 pounds, was quicker than he appeared, but his calm gait connoted a lack of hustle to the untrained eye.

The "trained eyes," college lacrosse coaches and scouts, were in the stands to see two All-State players from Perry Hall and Dulaney—neither of whom was Walsch.

Mike scored one goal and two assists and controlled the ball smartly throughout the game.

After the game, I spoke to Walsch. I introduced him to Kelly, and then explained our lacrosse program, the opportunity to play as a freshman against top competition, and the financial aid package. Although he acted noncommittal, I detected some interest. I also noticed that no other coaches or scouts had approached Walsch.

"What do you think, George?" I asked as we walked over to the parking lot.

"I'm amazed. Walsch is like the "Invisible Man." Everybody watched those two All-State midfielders go at each other and nobody noticed Walsch. He plays up to his competition. The better or harder you defend him, the better he'll be. If he comes to Morgan, we'll toughen him up. But I don't think he'll come."

"Why not?" I asked as we slid into my Datsun station wagon.

"He's too Waspy-lookin'"said Kelly. "Got that blondish-brown hair and blue-eyed preppy look—much different than Andi and Courtenay. The boy looks like he belongs at University of Virginia or somewhere Ivy."

Walsch may have appeared preppy, but his roots were blue-collar. His dad was a machinist/mechanic from the city who moved his family to White Marsh in far eastern Baltimore County in the mid-fifties.

One of Mike's elementary school teachers was a former Hopkins lacrosse graduate, who taught the kids lacrosse in the fifth grade. Recreation Council leagues were formed, and Walsch teamed with his older brother until high school. He played two years of varsity lacrosse at Perry Hall and was named to the All-Baltimore County Second Team.

Vacillating over whether to even go to college, Mike found Morgan's offer of a free education appealing. He was also intrigued over the opportunity to compete immediately against the Bears' competitors, confident that he could start as a freshman.

○

Scott was playing basketball after practice on a playground near his home. Suddenly, a kid with a gun came onto the court and began shooting it up because he couldn't get into the game. One of the bullets ricocheted off the cement, wounding Scott in the foot.

I called Doctor Becker. "I need you to see one of my players right away for a serious lacrosse injury."

"Meet me at my office," replied Becker.

At the office, Dr. Becker came out of the examining room incredulous and asked, "What kind of lacrosse injury? I just took a bullet out of his foot!"

I explained what had truly happened, and Becker just shook his head.

"It is theoretically a lacrosse injury because it happened after practice, but before he got home," I insisted.

○

Before the Adelphi game, their coach told me that they couldn't play because half of their game jerseys were missing. Immediately, I sought out Scott, who, speaking for the team, said, "They're just souvenirs, Coach."

"Okay," I said, "but take 'em *after* the game!"

I returned the jerseys and the game proceeded.

Tyrone "Puddie" Jones racing downfield against Adelphi University.

O

Mendoza Wallace, a very fine Morgan defenseman from Farmingdale Community College, wore an allergy mask when playing; a look that scared the hell out of opposing players. He played great against Adelphi (and all season long), but Morgan lost 14 to 4. The Bears finished the 1974 season ranked tenth in Division II out of eighty teams, but failed to make the eight-team tournament. Had we beaten Adelphi we would have been selected, but the Bears couldn't even win a face-off that day. Puddie played poorly, and he took the loss personally.

O

Mendoza was a "homeboy" of Dave Raymond's. He shared Dave's apartment and, to keep him out of trouble, took the credit for all the girls Millie thought were seeing Dave.

Mendoza Wallace's family came from Kingston, Jamaica. They moved to Brooklyn when he was a tot, and by the time he turned twelve, they had moved to Hempstead, Long Island. An excellent athlete, Mendoza ran track and played lacrosse and football.

Defenseman Mendoza Wallace (wearing allergy mask) on the ground as he makes a pass against Loyola.

After high school, Mendoza attended Farmingdale Community College where he made Junior College All-American as a defenseman, even though he had played midfield when he was at Hempstead High with Dave Raymond. Mendoza had a scholarship offer to attend Roanoke College, but declined and came to Morgan instead after I was able to get him an athletic scholarship at the last moment. Mendoza wanted to play with his friend Dave, and was also waiting for Mug Hunt and Billy "Maceo" Mayfield, their other buddies, to join them for the following season at Morgan State.

Mendoza was very "close" with his cash. He had grown up in a household where there wasn't a lot of money, and everyone hoarded what they had. As a matter of fact, his parents *always* locked their room. There was a lot of independence and not a great deal of trust in the household growing up. That's how Mendoza evolved—always hoarding things. Even as Dave's Morgan State roommate in an apartment off campus, he would lock his room.

Mendoza never loaned anything to anyone, either. Very frugal, he saved every penny and brought his life savings with him to Morgan.

During practice and games, he wore allergy masks due to a severe grass pollen allergy. Whenever Mendoza became allergic, his eyes swelled shut and he developed an angry streak.

Mendoza had a hopped-up Chevy Nova with struts that kept the rear end very high. He didn't let anyone ride in the backseat because he didn't want to affect the way the struts performed. So, only he and Dave, and maybe one other person, could squeeze into the front seat. One time, on the way to classes, there were two students they knew hitchhiking to the college. Mendoza stopped, but picked up only one to squeeze in the front with him and Dave, stringently upholding the "no backseat" rule.

One afternoon outside the Student Union, a car backed into Mendoza's prized Nova denting the front door. He went crazy, and a physical argument ensued. Mendoza pulled out a huge pipe from the trunk of the car and began fighting with five or six guys. A teammate, Gerald Nesbit, saw the fight and ran over to the gymnasium to get Dave Raymond, George Kelly, and some of the other lacrosse team members. They ran back to protect Mendoza, who was now holding off at least a dozen people by swinging the long iron pipe wildly.

O

Ochiki Young was the first inmate to receive a college degree while incarcerated in a state prison. He completed his senior year of college, earning a bachelor's degree in health science.

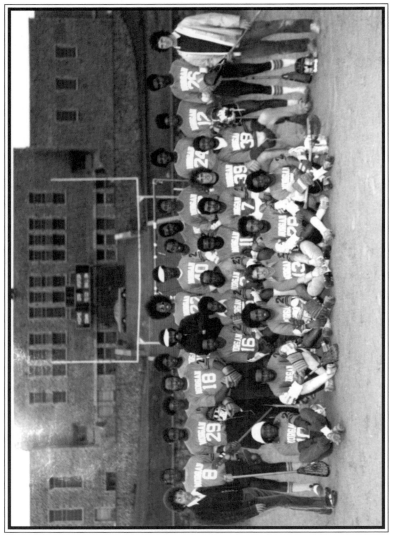

The 1974 Morgan State Lacrosse Team.

CHAPTER 9

TEN BEARS, ONE TEAM: MORGAN STATE'S ARRIVAL

SUMMER 1974

At a team meeting at the end of the season as the players were returning their equipment, I was lecturing on the opportunities that would open up to black lacrosse players as a result of playing the game and being part of a close-knit fraternity of the lacrosse world in Baltimore.

My predictions for bright futures and numerous opportunities were in stark contrast with the actual summer jobs of the players.

"You'll eventually find yourselves on top of the business community . . ."

Raymond and Mendoza were tarring the rooftop of a downtown building.

"Doors will open, socially and culturally . . ."

Two players were cleaning out a bathroom stall with one holding open the stall door.

"The corridors of the upper-crust establishment will be available . . ."

A player was cleaning the hallways and corridors of an all-white country club.

"And kids from all walks of life will look up to you . . . You'll be role models . . ."

Andi and Bacon were being hassled and teased by kids at Camp Concern. And kids in a loft watched Andi screw his girlfriend, while Bacon sold obsolete military furniture and equipment to civilian secondhand shops.

○

The players were once again participating in the summer league. They were having a greater impact because they had picked up additional skills over the previous years. The summer league gave them the opportunity to participate alongside players from top college teams, and they became friendly with Towson's Darkie Darcangelo and W & L's Jack Dudley, both All-Americans.

Sheldon Freed, the Bears' defense coach, was planning to attend dental school in August. But instead of honing up for his grueling first-year classes, he decided to coach in the summer league. He was responsible for drafting a number of Morgan State players, including Kelly, Dink, and Scott.

The summer league teams had co-coaches, and Sheldon's was G. Darrell Russell, a white attorney, who also coached at Loyola College. The first game of the season was poorly played and the team lost. Around that time, Sheldon rethought his priorities and opted for a chemistry refresher course, leaving the team under the sole tutelage of Coach Russell. Although unfamiliar with coaching black players, Darrell struck a common chord and was able to win every game following the first loss, leading the team into the championship finale.

During the title game, a number of fights broke out, and Coach Russell was arguing with the referees about some questionable calls. Several opposing players surrounded Darrell, jostling him. George Kelly came to the rescue, laying out four guys before Coach Russell advised, "George, that's enough. I think we've made our point."

○

All summer long Puddie brooded over his season of injuries. He accepted the blame for Morgan missing the tournament and pledged to himself that he'd improve. He played in the summer league and was on the same team as Scott and the guys. It was there that he really began to hone his skills.

During the summer nights he would go with Dink, Scott, and Jacques to O'Dell's, a disco on North Avenue in downtown Baltimore. It was the spot to party. The guys dressed around ten p.m., arrived at eleven p.m., and partied until two a.m. During the day,

Puddie worked at Sparrows Point, which was owned by Bethlehem Steel. He was part of the 406 Labor Gang on the steel side as opposed to the shipbuilding side. They did furnace repair, taking firebrick out of blast mills and making steel beams. It was hard work, but it paid well. There were bricklayers who would replace these bricks, but this was not one of Puddie's jobs.

Actually, Dink did that type of work. Every summer, he worked at Harbison-Walker, a Pittsburgh-based company that serviced steel mills, making and replacing firebrick for Sparrows Point Shipyard.

O

The Baltimore Colts were very happy with Cherry's first year of pro football. But then came a players' strike in the NFL. Cherry was not in the players' union, but he refused to cross the picket line because of his friendships with Ray Chester and Lydell Mitchell. General Manager Thomas was very upset with Cherry, feeling betrayed after he had given him such a big break. Thomas traded him to the Jets, where he was reunited with the same linebacker coach from the Patriots who had previously cut him.

FALL 1974

At the first day of fall practice, new recruit Mike Walsch watched the other players show up late and hungover. I ordered a mile run, which Walsch was sure he'd win. However, the players all beat him by a full lap, disillusioning him initially, and then elating him.

Maybe these guys are better than I figured, thought Walsch.

I put Mendoza on Walsch during the first scrimmage and ordered him to play Walsch hard. Mike responded well and held his own. This helped him gain immediate respect.

Over the next two weeks, Walsch was befriended by Kelly and looked after by Courtenay. Lacrosse was the easy part for Mike at Morgan during his first month of college. It was the classroom side that was overwhelming and intimidating. Mike endured a great deal of taunting because he was white. Had it not been for lacrosse, he would have most certainly dropped out.

"It seems everyone is watching me," Mike told Courtenay. "I stand out in every class."

"Really?" asked Courtenay. "I never felt that. But, then again, I'm only five-feet-three."

During the first semester of the '74-'75 academic year, controversy raged on campus over the desire of Morgan State to achieve university status. No matter what the course, the topic always came up in class.

In Walsch's Introduction to Psychology class, the professor was discussing whether Morgan wanted to be a great black university or just a great university. A student, pointing to Mike, called out, "Look at this guy. Why is he here?"

Mike didn't know what to say, but before he could respond the professor said, "You all don't get it. This is not a white versus black issue."

Later, when confronted about his reason for being at Morgan, Walsch developed "pat" answers depending upon the intimidation factor. It was either "To get an education," "To play lacrosse," or "Because it's free."

○

In a surprise move, Governor Marvin Mandel granted parole to Irving H. "Ochiki" Young. Over 20,000 people had petitioned the governor, who commuted Ochiki's life sentence following a meeting with him the week before.

Had the Governor not acted, Ochiki would not have been eligible for parole for another 17 years.

○

I had four prized recruits: Walsch, Joe Fowlkes, Tom Scott, and Wendell "Blizzard" Z. (Zee). I asked Wendell, "Why do they call you the Blizzard?"

Wendell, looking menacingly at me, answered, "'Cause I chill people!"

Wendell drove an old Buick convertible and always wore sunglasses.

Joe Fowlkes looked like the quintessential athlete at 6'2" tall, 200 pounds, and with a chiseled build. He was an All-State football and lacrosse player from Baltimore City's Walbrook High School. Joe dreamed of playing football at Morgan, but the coaches were no longer impressed with Baltimore's scholastic football programs and depended heavily on New Jersey and Texas recruits.

I begged new head football coach Nat Turner to give Fowlkes

a tryout. (Turner replaced Banks, who had retired from football but remained as the athletic director.)

"He's a great offensive threat," I said. "He can play flanker, kick field goals and extra points, and return kickoffs."

Turner pondered my request while staring at Fowlkes' red football shoes.

"Tell ya what, Chip," he said. "I'll give him a shot at defensive back, but he's gotta lose the shoes!"

○

On an unusually cold late October afternoon, Morgan played Johns Hopkins, the team with more national championships than any other. The Bears almost beat Hopkins in the scrimmage. Everyone was sorry to see fall lacrosse end, but sensed that in the coming spring season they were going to have one hell of a team.

During the Hopkins game, Mike Walsch played on the first attack unit with Dave Raymond and John Workman. After a sluggish freshman year, Workman had made great strides both in lacrosse athleticism and confidence.

Dave Raymond scoring against Johns Hopkins University in a fall scrimmage.

The chilly weather had the players wearing long-sleeve shirts and sweatpants. On the sidelines, fans huddled closely on the windswept field.

Sandy, Mike's high school sweetheart, stood between Mike's dad and her father watching the closely played fall scrimmage.

"Which one is Mike?" asked Sandy's dad. Incredulous as the question sounded, white Walsch was indistinguishable due to the helmet, uniform, and equipment.

Mike waved to Sandy as he stood outside of the huddle listening to my instructions. Big mistake. Scott and some of the other guys noticed.

"Better not let her near me," warned Dink, "'cause if I ever get a hold of her, you'll never see her again."

"Here," added Scott, "wear my cup. She'll think you have a big dick!"

○

It was intriguing to watch George Kelly evolve into an excellent defenseman. Slowly and steadily, season to season, he had improved dramatically. By his final season, he could either shut out or take the opposing top attackman out of just about every game. We even took for granted his greatest feat. It wasn't until years later that we understood the enormity of it.

Mike O'Neil was a freshman sensation playing for Johns Hopkins in the fall of 1974 in a scrimmage game played against the Bears on a back practice field on the storied grounds of Homewood. After four quarters, the game was tied, so the teams played an extra ten minutes of extra-man offense and defense, which the Bears had not practiced all fall. Hopkins won the game, but Morgan dominated. George Kelly took O'Neil totally out of the game, and it so disillusioned O'Neil that he considered dropping out of school. The coaches convinced him otherwise, and he went on to become a brilliant multiyear All-American for Johns Hopkins University.

○

At Dave Raymond's apartment, Millie dropped by unexpectedly. Dave opened the door in a robe and sat with Millie on the sofa. Suddenly, a girl emerged from the bedroom straightening her skirt, and walked out the front door.

"Wow, I never even saw her come in," said Dave. "Must be a friend of Mendoza's."

○

By his sophomore year, Puddie realized a college degree wasn't his priority. He did not apply himself and wasn't much of a student. He loved to play ball, though. And at Morgan, he especially loved the good times.

Puddie and the guys were enthused about the opportunity to play Hopkins and University of Maryland in the fall, and holding their own against two premier programs. The guys were starting to realize how good they were. They even had a feeling that they could possibly knock off Washington and Lee the following spring. Every Thursday night, they met at Dave Raymond's and talked about winning and what would be necessary to accomplish it.

O

Camilla "Millie" Yates, Miss Morgan, 1975. *(photo:* Promethean 1975, *Morgan State College Yearbook)*

Millie took part in a major sit-in on campus to protest Morgan not receiving university status. The students blocked Hillen Road and Cold Spring Lane. The riot police came with dogs and in riot gear, but nothing escalated. The spokespeople, including Millie, kept the crowd calm.

Even after her involvement in the sit-in, Millie was elected Miss Morgan for the '74-'75 academic year. In her acceptance speech at the Fine Arts Center, Millie spoke of the importance of the campus being supportive of and focusing on the sports teams.

"For example," she said, "the lacrosse team needs a lot of community involvement and school support. Do you understand the importance of having the only black lacrosse team in America?"

She was booed by the student crowd, who felt that athletic teams took too much of Morgan's money to begin with.

O

Mike Walsch sat in chemistry class listening to the instructor.

"If you spill silver nitrate on your skin, it'll turn black." Jokingly, the instructor added, "Care to come up and try it, Mr. Walsch?"

The class and Mike laughed. Tyrone Scott, who was auditing the class so he could be with his girlfriend, Boots, called out, "He'll still need new hair, cooler clothes, a different walk, and slicker talk."

Walsch took all the kidding and intimidation in stride now. He was part of the Ten Bears and enjoyed being on the periphery of his popular teammates. Although some were a bit loud and obnoxious, the lacrosse players basked in the same limelight as the football and basketball stars.

WINTER 1974-75

At the annual lacrosse convention, W & L Coach Emmer sought me out to play Morgan once again in the season opener. I readily agreed.

SPRING 1975

I had finally gotten Marvin Webster out onto the practice field. The "Human Eraser" had a stick and was shooting the ball from the crease as Raymond fed him. At seven feet tall, no one could stop him. All he had to do was catch the ball.

○

"All right, let's go over the High Post Offense, again," I ordered as the players groaned. They'd been practicing it for forty-five minutes a day for two weeks.

My forte was psychology—my only innovative regimen to the game of lacrosse. Basically, I stole practice routines, plays, and game strategies from other teams and coaches and adapted them to fit Morgan. The teams I copied from the most were University of Maryland, Johns Hopkins University, and Navy. And the High Post Offense, developed by Coach Bud Beardmore from Maryland, was my favorite. (Lots of cuts and picks with variations from the same set.)

Although George Kelly and Tyrone Scott were on opposite ends of the spectrum personality-wise, they played lacrosse more for the fun of it than anything else. And they enjoyed the team camaraderie considerably. However, after two seasons playing in the Hero Summer Lacrosse League and playing Fall Ball against perennial powers Hopkins, Navy, and Maryland, the game took on a new meaning. They realized that the Ten Bears were good enough to play at any level, and win!

Attackman John Workman (#27) dodging from behind the goal against the University of Baltimore.

◯

A week before traveling to W & L, the Bears scrimmaged the University of Baltimore, my alma mater. We hadn't played the Bees in a regular season game since 1971. They were a perennial Division II tournament selection. The Bears won 13 to 3, even though I kept three starters out of the game due to minor ailments.

◯

As my coaching philosophy shaped up over the years, I became obsessed with scouting reports on opposing teams. At first I'd call friendly coaches for their scouting reports, then I'd send out Schnoo or some injured players. Finally, consumed with the importance of the reports, I began to scout teams myself, leaving Schnoo or others to conduct practice. Sometimes, I'd call off a practice and take the entire team with me, and we'd all scout an opponent.

I designed my own reporting system. I had information on every play, ride, clear, defense, extra man, and so on, plus a review of every player's strengths, weaknesses, and attitude. Sometimes it paid off and other times it proved meaningless, but I swore by it. Days before every game, each player was given a copy of the entire report on the current opponent.

The only time a scouting report couldn't be put together was at the beginning of a season when there had been no games to scout. This was always the case for the first game with W & L, but I had a plan.

Frequently, I went to STX, a lacrosse equipment outlet, where I had gotten friendly with Tom George, a former Washington College star attackman. Tom worked in the store and was also playing club ball for Carling Lacrosse Club, which scrimmaged Washington and Lee the same day the Bears scrimmaged University of Baltimore.

The Monday before the W & L game, I took off work and spent three hours at STX with Tom George going over W & L. When I was finished, I had 60 pages of notes.

◯

I received an additional scouting report, albeit brief, from an old friend named Joe Harlan, a club lacrosse All-Star, also playing for the Carling Lacrosse Club. I played against Joe when he attended Friends School in the late '50s. Later, Joe was a teammate of mine on the University of Maryland freshman lacrosse team, and a fellow defenseman of Schnoo Snyder's for two years.

In 1963, when I was ineligible due to transferring from the University of Maryland to the University of Baltimore, I played with the University Club lacrosse team sponsored by a private club in center-city Baltimore. The University Club Collegians was an outgrowth of a summer box lacrosse team that included numerous graduating All-Americans. These players convinced the University Club to sponsor a team since they did not want to play for the older, established club lacrosse teams, such as Mt. Washington, Maryland, and Baltimore Lacrosse Club. Regardless of how good one was coming out of college, tenure had to be earned and a "pecking order" followed before starting and seeing a lot of action for these teams.

So the University Club team was born in the spring of 1963 and consisted of many graduating seniors who would go on to be major coaches in the game of lacrosse for the next dozen years, including the head coaches at University of Maryland, Johns Hopkins, the Naval Academy, Hobart, Washington and Lee, Princeton, UCLA, and other fine schools. Even though I ended up running on the sixth midfield and seeing very little action, I learned more about lacrosse being on that team than I'd ever imagined.

Interestingly, the University Club had never had any Jews in its membership. It was a restricted club. Ironically, they decided to give membership to all of the players of the new club lacrosse team, not realizing that five were Jewish.

That 1963 University Club team won the U.S. Open Lacrosse title defeating a great Mt. Washington team 8 to 6.

The University Club stopped sponsoring the team in the late '60s, and the Carling Brewery, which brewed beer on the western side of the Baltimore Beltway, took up sponsorship of the team.

O

I went over the scouting report of the Washington and Lee Generals with the Bears until they were familiar with every play and player. Then I devised a strategy.

W & L was solid everywhere. Although they may not have been as strong as in the past two years, they had depth and skills that were as good as any team playing lacrosse currently, except for perhaps the University of Maryland, which was returning a team that had won the NCAA championship in '73, lost in the finals in '74, but looked to repeat in '75.

The true strength of Washington and Lee was in two returning All-American defensemen, Tom Keigler and Rob Lindsay. They were big, strong, fast, and had outstanding stickwork. W & L also ran three midfields; two of equal strength and a third that could be used to give the first two midfields time to regroup. Their attack was lead by a transfer from the Air Force Academy named Donnie Carroll, who was probably their fastest player. Fortunately, for the Bears, returning All-American Dave Warfield was injured and not available to play against Morgan.

Using my "scouting report," I evaluated the Washington and Lee offensive plays and defensive sets, and worked the Bears overtime so that they were prepared for any move that W & L might make. I did not expect Coach Emmer to play his team much differently against my Morgan squad than how he had played them against the Carling Lacrosse Club in the scrimmage the week before.

○

The W & L squad had many returning lettermen from the team that destroyed Morgan 16 to 4 in 1974. However, there was a sleeker, quicker, more skilled Morgan "10" coming down in March of 1975 that would totally surprise the Generals. Perhaps they'd heard of Morgan's good showing against Johns Hopkins in Fall Ball, or certainly they knew how the Bears had taken apart a supposedly strong University of Baltimore team in a scrimmage while holding back three starters; but I did not think that that information would be enough for Washington and Lee to totally alter any strategy going into the game.

The Bears' defense was more solid than it had ever been. Courtenay was back for his fourth year in the goal, finally realizing he was never going to run midfield. He had twice been named to the All-American team. He was considered one of the finest goalies in the country, Division I or Division II; and now he was surrounded by a very quick, strong, and savvy defense that had some depth. George Kelley and Mendoza Wallace played the back line, and on the crease, Paige Beckwith and Aaron Glover rotated their position. They all had good stickwork, and Glover's development had been truly amazing.

In the midfield, Morgan could throw three fast, solid units against W & L for the first time. Before, I had only been able to stack and play two midfields against such strong powers.

On attack, I had returning All-American Dave Raymond, the leading goal scorer for the Bears; sophomore crease attackman John Workman from Uniondale in Long Island; and my new freshman sensation, Mike Walsch, from Perry Hall High. There was even depth on attack with New Jersey's Ralph Anderson seeing lots of action.

After analyzing W & L's strengths and weaknesses over and over again, the strategy came down to this: I told each attackman that instead of Workman only playing crease attack (that is, in front of the goal) that Morgan would use a revolving attack, which meant that Raymond, Walsch, and Workman would play every attack position. Whichever attackman was being guarded by Washington and Lee's crease defenseman, a very good but lumbering young man, that attackman would take him behind the goal and force him to guard a dodger. I wanted my players to avoid having to dodge around Keigler and Lindsay, fast and aggressive defensemen. So Morgan's offensive strategy was simply to force W & L's defensemen to play out of position.

A second key strategy revolved around Washington and Lee's "clear," that is, bringing the ball up from their defensive zone. Instead of a zone "ride," Raymond and Workman would guard Keigler and Lindsay tightly and cut them off from getting the ball. The Bears would zone W & L's clearing defenseman, goalie, and midfielders with Walsch and the middies. This would be no easy task since Keigler and Lindsay were excellent clearers and could bring the ball up using their great speed and dodging ability. By keeping them from the ball on the clear, Morgan would be able to keep Washington and Lee in their defensive zone much longer. So, our primary offensive and defensive strategies revolved around the Washington and Lee defense.

○

The Bears were in the greatest shape they had ever been in, running in the snow since January, with wind sprints and long-distance endurance runs. I had adapted a practice regimen from the University of Maryland the year before and drilled it over and over again. Every day, all of the players would run a 300-yard dash, walk back to the starting line within 20 seconds, run 300 yards again, and then repeat it once more. I would record their averages and set a daily goal. After practice, the team would run one or two miles, depending on how practice went. Once a player met my required times in the dashes and distance, he'd be finished. The others ran for another month. This was the year that Morgan had the "horses." Nine of the midfielders seemed as if they could run all day, and run fast. Jacques was by far the fastest Bear, now that Oliver Chambers had graduated.

○

Jerna Jacques, the third member of the Gruesome Threesome, was born in west Baltimore. His family moved to northwest Baltimore when he was very young. He played Little League baseball at Howard Park and basketball in the Baltimore Neighborhood Basketball League. He attended Northwestern High and, as a junior, played receiver and defensive back on the varsity football team. He also played midfield on the varsity lacrosse team. Because he didn't have enough money to go to the junior prom, he only played three games during his junior year of varsity lacrosse. He quit the team to get a job in a restaurant as a dishwasher so he could earn enough money for the prom. However, he decided not to go when he could not find a "dream" date, and eventually rejoined the lacrosse team.

Jacques decided to attend Morgan State as a football walk-on; that is, someone who was not recruited but could try out for the team as long as the coaches approved. Because of his excellent speed and size, he was given an opportunity to participate. He made the practice squad immediately as a defensive back.

Jacques was promised a football scholarship if he made the team during spring football, but he didn't want to give up lacrosse. Plus, football practice in the fall and spring would tire him out too much, taking energy away from his partying around with Dink and Scott.

○

Dave Raymond and Mug Hunt (his buddy from Hempstead, Long Island) needed new shoes for the W & L game. I agreed to "foot" the bill and loaned them my credit card. I warned them to buy shoes and nothing else, no "hanky-panky." At a mall sporting goods store, they bought shoes, socks, jerseys, and sweat suits. Afterwards, they ordered $60 worth of carryout from a Chinese restaurant and charged that to my credit card, too.

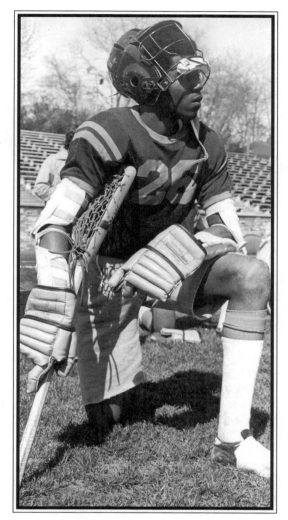

Midfielder Jerna Jacques.

○

   The night before the team left for W & L, they met for their pregame session at Raymond's apartment. This time the players painted their orange and blue helmets black to enhance their formidable looks, and vowed to play their finest game. They also feasted on a virtual banquet of Chinese food.

○

Before leaving for Washington and Lee, Marvin Webster predicted that the team would win the game. Basketball Coach Frazier waited by the bus anticipating that I would try to sneak Webster on board. The Bear basketball team had just returned from winning the NCAA small college championship, and Webster was predicted to be a first-round choice in the NBA or ABA draft.

Frazier was concerned that if Marvin tried to play lacrosse, he could be seriously injured and miss out on a financially rewarding pro basketball career.

○

I decided that there would be no curfew. The guys could go out on the town or play basketball until three in the morning. I didn't care.

The atmosphere at W & L was one of victory before battle. The students, not taking the match seriously, were celebrating beating Morgan even before the game began. The whole campus was partying. This urged the Morgan players on even more. They considered it a lack of respect. The only W & L student or player who seemed to have respect for Morgan was Jack Dudley, who had played with many of the guys in the summer league. He knew how good Morgan was and how seriously they needed to be taken. But he had trouble getting this across to his teammates. No one believed Jack's insistence that Morgan was a much better team than the one they pummeled 16 to 4 in 1974.

That evening, Mike Walsch was ushered around campus by a wealthy former Perry Hall High School classmate. Everywhere they went, W & L students did double takes when they heard Walsch was a Morgan State player. Walsch also took in their comments pertaining to the game:

"This is the easiest way to start the season."

"The toughest part of our schedule is later."

"Maybe we'll hold the score down since last year was such a blowout."

○

Puddie, Jacques, Scott, and Dink met some local blacks and followed them into the town of Lexington. One of the locals had a girlfriend at Morgan State, and he invited the guys to a party.

The black section of town was called "Soulville," and the party took place in the crowded living room of someone's home. Dink watched in amazement as Bubbie (now serving as an assistant coach) danced slowly with a big, fat girl, unable to get his hands around her rotund body.

The blacks of Lexington did not understand lacrosse and never went to a game. However, they chided the players with: "You all gonna get beat tomorrow." But Puddie retorted, "If you come to the game, we'll win!"

O

Some of the guys chose to let off steam by shooting hoops in the gym. Coach Emmer of W & L came by and smiled while watching the basketball games. I was also playing and getting "stuffed"(blocked) on every shot I took.

O

When the guys were finally in bed, Scott and Dink began throwing fruit in the dark. A peach hit Bullock, who at first was dangerously silent, but then announced that he needed to get up and "relieve himself," anyway. While he was in the men's room, Scott and Dink spread mayonnaise inside his sheets. When Bullock returned, he "slid" into the bed and started screaming that something inside his bed was pulling him under.

O

The team jogged from the visitors' dressing room at W & L across a bridge and into the stadium. Two unleashed German shepherds prowled the far side of the field, growling and barking at the Ten Bears.

"Scoop the ball cleanly over there," warned Mendoza Wallace, glancing toward the dogs. "It's sticks out front, body to the side, or them dogs'll tear you apart!"

Before the game, Puddie gazed up into the stands and saw an unusual sight—a group of blacks way up at the top of the upper deck. They were the same ones who were at the party. Puddie turned to some of the players and said, "Hey, guys, we gotta win because them 'town blacks' have shown up. We can't let 'em down."

Defenseman Mendoza Wallace (#38) and goalie Courtenay Servary block a W&L shot as Morgan defensemen George Kelly (#17) and Aaron Glover (#24) race to help.

The players stuck to the game plan and got the ball to Workman, Raymond, and Walsch. They set the offensive strategy into play. At one point early in the first quarter, Puddie dove in front of a sure goal and blocked the shot with his head. A fast break ensued and resulted in a Morgan goal. This ignited the Bears and took a bit of the spark out of the Washington and Lee Generals. Things were going well.

At the end of the first quarter, Coach Emmer was overheard asking his players, "What's wrong with you guys?"

In the huddle, the Bears felt confident. Scott yelled out, "We can win this game!" And, as usual, once Courtenay got through the first quarter, he "clicked" and got better.

As the game progressed, Scott and some of the other players were chiding the W & L midfielders that they were running the wrong plays, referring to them by their names, and befuddling them. The W & L players could not believe how well they'd been scouted, complaining to their coach that Morgan was anticipating every play.

We had a sizeable lead after three quarters. However, late in the fourth quarter Washington and Lee scored twice to close the gap to 8 to 7. I called a time-out. I realized my midfield unit of Puddie, Dink, and Jacques had been on the field for a long time and were tired. Still, it was the first game of the year, they were in

Midfielder Bernard Watkins (#23) chasing down a W&L middie.

great shape, and it was a chance at one of the greatest upsets in lacrosse history. I decided to keep them in after the time-out.

Throughout the game, George Kelly guarded the fleet Donnie Carroll and defended him well. Following a loose ball out-of-bounds before the final gun, George knew that Carroll would try and dodge around him with ten seconds left. As Carroll came flying around the goal for his shot, George knocked him down as he fired the ball. Courtenay made a phenomenal save, passing out afterwards from hyperventilating. Just then, the gun went off signaling the end of the game. The Ten Bears had won 8 to 7.

Goalie Courtenay Servary making a crucial save against Washington and Lee.

The guys were ecstatic. As the game ended, they threw their sticks in the air and danced on the field.

O

The Washington and Lee coach climbed onto the bus before the team left. He praised and congratulated the Bears.

"This was no upset or fluke. You guys are a great team!" exclaimed Coach Emmer, a class act.

EPILOGUE I

When the team arrived back in Baltimore, their win was being called by some "the greatest upset in the history of intercollegiate sports." There was extensive media coverage, letters of congratulation, and numerous phone calls to Athletic Director Banks and me from lacrosse aficionados across the country. The letter I cherished the most was from Bob Scott, the legendary Johns Hopkins head coach who had won more national championships than any other lacrosse coach (and had also graduated from Forest Park High School; Scott, Miles, and my alma mater).

At first, only the relatively small, close-knit lacrosse fraternity could comprehend the immensity of the victory over W & L. But, as the season progressed, word spread, and by the 1975 NCAA Division I Tournament, the win had taken on legendary proportions. In the quarterfinal round, W & L beat Johns Hopkins, adding to the legitimacy of the Morgan victory.

There were immediate changes in the manner in which the individual Ten Bears were treated. Dink, Scott, Jacques, and Puddie were riding on a metro bus on their way to school one day carrying lacrosse sticks. They were surprised at the outpouring of praise and recognition from people on the bus in the black community who were beginning to understand just what these players had accomplished.

Media coverage grew dramatically after the W&L victory. *(photo:* Baltimore Sunpapers, *Joseph A. DiPaulo)*

At a practice a couple of days after the W & L game, I told the players that I was concerned that this early victory could hurt the rest of the season, and that I would like to get to and win the Division II Tourney. "But," I added, "I wouldn't trade this win for anything!"

The rest of the '75 spring lacrosse season was anticlimatic, but went by in a surrealistic blur. There were many more fond memories and events that season, but all were far out-shadowed by that Saturday in early March in Lexington, Virginia.

However, looking back through the rest of March until mid-May 1975, there were moments . . .

● Harvard University came to play the Ten Bears. For the first time, Morgan's president and several of the vice presidents and department chairs were at a lacrosse game. Tiger Davis came out for old-times' sake as well. That Harvard had sent a team to play at Morgan was unbelievable to the academic side of the school. Even Coach Banks, who seldom spoke to the players, pulled up Dave Raymond and encouraged him to beat Harvard.

Like many visiting teams that came to Morgan, Harvard was intimidated, especially in the student cafeteria. However, on the field, before the game, they became cocky. After the game began, though, they saw Morgan's prowess and the intimidation returned.

Harvard had a black goalie from Baltimore and the guys tormented him. Dave Raymond scored a couple of goals with time running out to seal a 9 to 7 victory for Morgan.

Dave Raymond scoring one of his goals against Harvard.
(photo: Baltimore Sunpapers, William Hotz)

As the game ended, Tiger approached the new Morgan State College president. "You ain't been here before. Were you here for the struggle of these young men for the last five years, or is it because Harvard University just happens to be playing?"

As successful as the Ten Bears were, many in the Athletic Department still had nothing but bad words for the lacrosse team—constantly accusing them of unsportsmanlike behavior—like bad manners and cursing. Actually, to some extent that was true, but a lot of it was jealousy. Many of Morgan's other teams (except for basketball) were in a down cycle. The lacrosse team was winning, going to the NCAA Tourney, getting excellent media attention, and beating "name" all-white colleges.

● Two hours before the Wittenberg game, the players gathered at Dave's for a session. Too many drank a lot and some smoked reefer. More than a few got so wasted that they were barely able to get to the game, let alone play.

Shockingly, the undefeated Morgan team lost to Wittenberg College 5 to 4, even though they totally dominated play between the goals. Wittenberg's goalie stopped almost every shot. And the Bears actually outshot them by 51!

The first night of Passover was held at my house and occurred right after the loss to Wittenberg. "Wigged-out" over the loss, I screwed up the traditional prayers and passages. Family members were aghast at my behavior.

● The Bears ran off five straight wins and were 9 and 1 going into an away game against a vastly improving Delaware team. We lost. Returning home, a group of players were smoking marijuana in the rear of the team bus, and I decided to make some changes. I switched the lineup to motivate the players. One, Wendell the Blizzard was demoted, and he told Scott that he was going to beat me up. Scott called Cherry and alerted him to the threat.

At the next day's practice, Wendell confronted me. He badmouthed and even shoved me. I told him he was off the team, and as the Blizzard drew back to punch me, he suddenly stopped and began to apologize profusely.

Unbeknownst to me, Cherry was standing behind me, staring menacingly at Wendell. I went back down to practice, never seeing Cherry who had put his arm around Wendell and walked off with him. Wendell never returned to Morgan.

● Tiger Davis dropped out of graduate school without completing the final requirements for his degree. I pulled him aside one day and insisted that he finish his thesis so that he could receive his master's degree from the school. For months, I was relentless until Tiger finally wrote the paper and graduated.

● Ochiki Young became an employee of the Baltimore Community Relations Board. He also enrolled in a graduate program in psychology.

● In the next three games, Morgan beat Georgetown, but was soundly trounced by UMBC and Towson State, barely hanging on to be selected to the Division II Tournament.

I was awaiting the Registrar's Eligibility List needed before the team went to play in the Division II Tournament against Washington College again.

"It's amazing that this is the only sport that has never had an academically ineligible player in all the years it's been in operation," exclaimed an assistant registrar.

Then the assistant registrar mentioned that a couple of players had African and Muslim names similar to other students.

"Better that than some of the nicknames the kids have had," I said, "like Monk, Dink, Blizzard, Poopie, Puddie, Bubbie, Jelly Roll, and all sorts of others."

● Because Morgan lost a couple of games toward the end of the schedule, and competing teams began winning, we weren't sure that we would be selected to the NCAA Division II Tourney. Therefore, after the last regular season game, which ended earlier than most other teams, we did not practice for a week. Had we practiced, perhaps things would have been different in the tournament. I always felt that had the team lost to W & L, we could have possibly won or gone far in the Tourney. But I never regretted it. To me, beating W & L was better than winning the NCAA Tournament.

● Washington College defeated the Bears convincingly in the first round of the playoffs. At the end of the game, I told the guys how great the season was, and announced that I would not be returning.

Cherry was at the game, and after hearing that I was retiring, embraced me and told me that he loved me. Cherry announced to the players that even in defeat they should celebrate my efforts; so he lifted me into the air and began to carry me around the field on his left shoulder.

After a few minutes, Scott yelled up to Cherry, "Put him down, you fool, or these Eastern Shore people will think you're kidnapping a white man, and they'll start shootin' that cannon at us."

"Scott, Dink . . . I been looking for you two," said Cherry. He dropped me and started chasing them all over the field.

1975 Morgan State College Lacrosse Team.

EPILOGUE II

. . . Morgan State University continued to field a lacrosse team coached by Sheldon Freed for five years after I left, never having another winning season. They did, however, beat Notre Dame.

In the '90s, Notre Dame became a perennial NCAA Division I Tournament team and lacrosse power; however, they were struggling during the late '70s and early '80s. Still, to Morgan State, Notre Dame was synonymous with winning sports tradition. When Donnie Brown scored the decisive goal in the Bears' 13 to 12 overtime win, pandemonium reigned.

A wealthy Notre Dame alumnus watching the game and subsequent celebration became so distraught that he rushed over to the coach and offered a one million dollar donation to the program so the "Fighting Irish" would never again lose to Division II teams like Morgan.

● Joe Fowlkes, my last recruit, became a three-time All-American and graced the cover of *The Lacrosse Guide*, the bible of lacrosse enthusiasts, coaches, and players. Coach Banks dropped the program after 1980 due to budgetary constraints in the Athletic Department. Four of Coach Freed's former players: Joe Fowlkes, Jason Green, Donnie Brown, and Gene White coached middle and high school black lacrosse teams.

● Of the 100-plus student/athletes who played lacrosse for me from 1970 to 1975, over 70 percent received their college degrees, albeit some taking longer than the four- or five-year term. All are gainfully and successfully employed, and, most of all, they still maintain that camaraderie they developed as members of the Ten Bears.

○

Players from the 1970 - 1975 teams at a Ten Bears Reunion in 1996. *(photo: Howard Blumenfeld)*

As for what happened to those individuals featured in *Ten Bears* and a number of others who were members of the teams . . .

● Stanley Cherry, after brief stints as an NFL player for the Colts and Jets, became a correctional officer at the state penitentiary. He died under suspicious circumstances in 1993.

● Tiger Davis, Tony Fulton, and Curt Anderson were elected to the Maryland Legislature. In 1979, Tiger ran for Mayor of Baltimore City against popular incumbent William Donald Schaefer and was soundly defeated. He still represents the east Baltimore district in the legislature. Tony represents west Baltimore, and Curt returned to full-time practice as an attorney in Baltimore City.

● George Kelly is a 20-year veteran of the Baltimore City Police Department, after serving four years in the Army. He has a short time to go before retirement.

● Three-time All-American Joe Fowlkes is a security consultant who played defensive back in the NFL. He also coached several championship middle school lacrosse teams.

● Tyrone Hall is a physical education teacher in Burlington, North Carolina.

● Aaron Glover is a Lieutenant Colonel in the Air Force.

● Dink Brown and Billie Johns are with the Baltimore City and County Fire Departments, respectively.

● Gerald Nesbit, Ralph Anderson, Jason Green, and Bernard Watkins are computer programmers and consultants.

● Tyrone Scott is Facilities Director of Beth Am Synagogue. He married Boots and they have a daughter.

● Courtenay Servary, a two-time All-American, is an elementary school assistant principal. The two elderly brothers who let him live on their property left him their 145-acre farm when they died. Courtenay is married and has two children.

● Three-time All-American Wayne Jackson is football and basketball coach at Northwestern High School. In 1977, he married Nikki and has three children. He and his wife have been together since their first date in 1966.

● John Bacon is a human resources consultant. He married Barbria and has two sons. They now reside in North Carolina.

● Dickie Hall retired from the Army, works for Maryland's Juvenile Services Department, and referees lacrosse games.

● Andi Arenson is a history teacher in New York State and former head lacrosse coach at Vassar. He was touched and surprised at the number of former teammates who came to his mother's funeral in 1979.

● Tony Bullock is stage manager for Whitney Houston.

● Frank Woke is a science teacher at Northern High School.

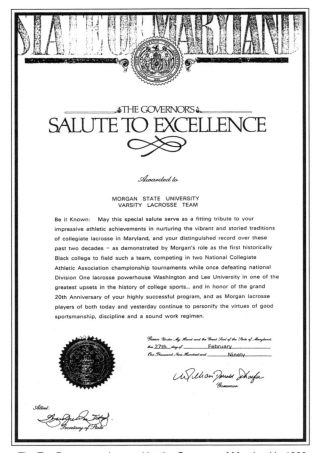

The Ten Bears were honored by the Governor of Maryland in 1990.

● William "Bubbie" Bennett is an executive with the Giant Food chain.

● Dave Raymond, a two-time All-American, North/South All-Star Game selection, and all-time leading Morgan scorer, married Millie and moved to Atlanta. He owns a large courier service and still plays club lacrosse.

● Millie Raymond is a manager for CIBA Vision Group, an international company, in the Applied Science and Manufacturing Technology Division.

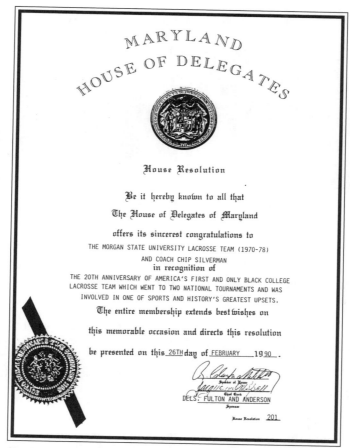

Maryland House of Delegates Resolution honoring the Ten Bears on their Twentieth Anniversary.

● Mug Hunt owns a carpet business in Long Island.

● G. Darrell Russell, the summer league coach, became a judge in Baltimore County, Maryland.

● Mendoza Wallace is an insurance agent and owner of a taxi franchise in Hempstead, Long Island.

● Maurice Ashe is a steelworker at Republic Engineering Steel Corporation.

The Ten Bears are honored by the Maryland Legislature in 1990.

● Billy Murphy, the attorney who represented "The Morgan Four," ran for mayor and lost, became a judge, and then returned to practicing law. Today, he is considered the top criminal attorney in the Baltimore/Washington area.

● Oliver Chambers moved to Trinidad and disappeared while sailing in the Caribbean in 1988.

● Puddie Jones, an All-American, is a correctional officer in Jessup, Maryland.

● Maurice Wood is Regional Grand Lecturer at Most Worshipful Prince Hall, Grand Lodge, State of Maryland.

● George Pritchett is a Specialist in Management and Student Control in the Anne Arundel County, Maryland school system.

● Blaine White is an attorney in Washington D.C.

● Jack Reed is an elementary school teacher.

● Gregory Covington is Manager of Application Development and Support for W.R. Grace & Company, North America.

● David Porter is a CIA agent (whereabouts classified).

● Billy Mayfield is an undercover DEA agent (whereabouts classified).

● Jerna Jacques retired from the Air Force, is a longshoreman for Local 333 with the Port of Baltimore, and recently received his real estate license.

● Mike Walsch is Executive Vice President of Taneytown Bank & Trust in Western Maryland.

● Marvin Webster played pro basketball for several years, leading Seattle to the finals of the NBA Championship in 1978 before losing to the Washington Bullets. He finished his career with the New York Knicks.

● The photojournalists of the Ten Bears: DeWayne Wickham is a columnist for *USA Today*, an author, and a BET host; and Sid Brooks is a Three-Star General.

● Kweisi Mfume was not only able to get Morgan a radio station, but he became its first program director. Later he was a Baltimore City Councilman, a Maryland Congressman, head of the Congressional Black Caucus, and is now President of the NAACP.

● H. Rap Brown was paroled in 1976. He embraced Islam and became Jamil Abdullah Al-Amin. He moved to Atlanta, Georgia and opened a grocery store called The Community Store. A teacher and spiritual leader at Atlanta's West End Muslim Mosques, Al-Amin lectured at universities and Islamic organizations around the country. In 1995, a man who said Al-Amin shot him later recounted his story claiming that enforcement authorities pressured him into identifying the former militant.
However, in May of 2000, the former Black Panther leader was arrested for allegedly shooting two Atlanta sheriff's deputies, killing one. The deputies were tying to serve him with an arrest warrant on charges of receiving stolen goods and impersonating an officer.

● In 1997, Howard University became the only historically black college to field a women's lacrosse team.

● Jack Emmer coached at Washington & Lee for 11 years. His teams went to seven Division I NCAA Tournaments in his first eight years and beat in-state rival University of Virginia five straight times. Emmer took the head coaching position for Army at West Point in 1983 and has led Army to five tournament berths.

● W & L dropped out of Division I in the mid-eighties since it could no longer recruit for the high-caliber athletes being pursued by the bigger colleges with full scholarships. They now play in Division III.

● Dan "Schnoo" Snyder and Larry Levitt both died of cancer.

● Part-time face-off Assistant Coach Jerry Schnydman is now Assistant to the President of Johns Hopkins University.

● Coach Earl Banks died in 1993. He was inducted into five Sports Halls of Fame.

● President Jenkins died in a swimming pool accident in 1978.

● In the winter of 1990, twenty years after Morgan began its initial lacrosse season, the Ten Bears were honored by the Maryland legislature and the governor, and appeared in a *New York Times* sports page cover story.

TUESDAY, FEBRUARY 27, 1990
Copyright © 1990 The New York Times

Sports Pages

The New York Times

The 1978 Morgan State lacrosse team, which competed in the N.C.A.A. Division II tournament. Morgan State fielded a team from 1970 to 1980.

Honors for Offbeat Team That Shook Lacrosse

For 10 Years, Predominantly Black Morgan State Took On Tony Opponents With Spirit

By PHIL BERGER

● Syracuse Coach Roy Simmons Jr. guided the Orangemen to six national championships in the '80s and '90s . . .

A few years ago at an NBA exhibition game in the Carrier Dome at Syracuse between the Chicago Bulls and Los Angeles Lakers, the local equipment manager put in an emergency call to Roy Simmons Jr. at home.

"One of the players wants two lacrosse sticks for his sons. Can you bring them over as soon as possible?"

"There's too much traffic. I'll send them out Monday. Who are they for?" asked Roy Jr.

"Michael Jordan," answered the equipment manager.

MJ's sons were in a private school in Chicago where lacrosse had become very popular.

Was it the lacrosse exhibit in the Carrier Dome that precipitated the call from Jordan, or did he recall the beginning of the North Carolina lacrosse dynasty that developed when he attended college?

● In addition to Cherry and Poopie, Clyde Tatum, Danny Bell, and Leonard Spicer are dead. Clyde died of liver disease, Spicer was killed in an automobile accident returning to medical school, and two muggers murdered Bell in a robbery attempt.

We have dedicated this book to those five Bears.

● A March 21, 2000 *Washington Post* article written by Judith Evans, detailing the emergence of the Carroll lacrosse team, a Washington D.C. predominately black Catholic high school, quoted Jim Brown: "Cross-cultural experiences are good. It's educational. And I like inclusion. So naturally, I would love to see black people exposed to lacrosse and have the pleasure of that luxury."

ABOUT THE AUTHORS

Chip Silverman, Ph.D., M.P.H., M.S., C.A.S., was the coach of the Morgan State Bears from the team's inception through its remarkable 1975 season. He also returned briefly to coach the University of Baltimore to the 1977 national tournament. During that season he scheduled Morgan State, and soundly defeated them—a scenario which depressed him. In 1991 Chip was inducted into the Morgan State University Athletic Hall of Fame.

Silverman ran the State of Maryland Drug Abuse Administration for years, and later served as Vice President of Government Relations and Addiction Services for Magellan Health Services.

He has written four other books: *The Block* and *The Last Bookmaker* with Bob Litwin, *Aloha Magnum* with Larry Manetti, and *Diner Guys*.

O

Miles Harrison Jr., M.D., F.A.C.S., the Ten Bears' star attackman, was the first player selected from a black college to participate in the North/South All-Star Game in 1971. After graduating, he attended the University of Pennsylvania School of Medicine, and completed his surgical residency there.

Harrison returned to Baltimore in 1980 to private practice, and from 1991 to 1995 he was an Assistant Professor of Surgery at the University of Maryland School of Medicine. Presently he is on the full-time teaching faculty with the Sinai Hospital Surgical Associates, a teaching affiliate of the Johns Hopkins Surgical Residency Program. Dr. Harrison was also the founder of the breast cancer support group Sisters Surviving in 1991.

Miles' son, Kyle, an All-State selection in lacrosse during his junior year at Friends School, will play Division I lacrosse at Johns Hopkins University after graduating in 2001.